To my editor, Victoria, for never failing to improve on what I've written and for her boundless optimism.

- T. A.

To my agent, Susan, for cheering me on throughout this whole book.

- Y. I.

First published 2022 by Nosy Crow Ltd
Wheat Wharf, 27a Shad Thames
London, SE1 2XZ, UK

Nosy Crow Eireann Ltd
c/o Fieldfisher Ireland LLP
45 Mespil Road, Dublin 4,
D04 W2F1, Ireland

www.nosycrow.com

This edition published 2026

ISBN 978 1 80708 132 4

Nosy Crow and associated logos are trademarks and/or registered trademarks of Nosy Crow Ltd



A CIP catalogue record for this book is available from the British Library.

Printed in China following rigorous ethical sourcing standards.

1 3 5 7 9 8 6 4 2

# THE BIG BOOK OF MYSTERIES

TOM ADAMS • YAS IMAMURA

nosy crow

# CONTENTS

## DISAPPEARING PLACES



## SPIRITS AND GHOSTS



## MIND OVER MATTER

## INTELLIGENT ANCESTORS



## UNEXPLAINED OBJECTS

# INTRODUCTION

It might surprise you to discover that the world has many amazing mysteries that nobody can yet explain . . .

**What happened to the crew of the *Mary Celeste*? Did King Arthur really exist? And where are the Hanging Gardens of Babylon?**

We have dived to the bottom of the deepest oceans and scaled the highest mountains. We've braved barren deserts, trekked to remote jungles and even blasted off into the beyond. Technology has allowed us to explore our world in incredible detail. The same is true of our own bodies. Today, we know more about human beings than ever before. With the help of computers, we can peer inside our minds and watch memories being laid down, create new life in a laboratory and even connect, person to person, by thought alone.

These advances in science mean so much can be explained nowadays, so a good mystery will always capture our imaginations. And there are still some great ones out there . . .

Stonehenge. The Great Pyramid of Giza. The Antikythera mechanism. The Phaistos Disc. Structures and objects so incredible it's hard to believe our ancient ancestors built them. And yet they did. The evidence is clear for all to see. Great minds have puzzled over these finds for years, but they still leave us mystified.

So what about other kinds of mysteries? Things that are slightly harder to prove with solid evidence, like spirits and spooks. Or things that go bump in the night?

Long ago, humans made sense of the world through myths, folklore and legends. Before science explained so much, these stories may have helped people to understand life and death, and sickness and suffering. Stories of spirits from beyond the grave may have helped comfort our early ancestors when they lost a loved one. Creepy tales about creatures lurking in the woods might have warned them away from wild and dangerous places, and some of today's mysterious monsters, like the Yeti or Bigfoot, might be doing the same thing. Do ghost stories reveal our fear of the dark? Is our fascination with alien abductions a sign we are scared of strangers? Perhaps . . .

But you do need to be on your guard. Sometimes when you see something strange or if something incredible happens with no obvious explanation, it's easy to let your imagination get carried away. Remember, just because something appears to be extraordinary, it doesn't mean that it can never be explained. Put your emotions to one side, have a good hard look at the facts and with a bit of logic and reasoning, you might find a simple way to explain it.

When investigating these mysteries, always beware of false evidence. Today, we are surrounded by 'facts' – they're all over the internet, and we're fed them in bite-size chunks on social media. Even though something appears on the internet, or on the television, or even in a book, it's important to understand that it doesn't always mean it's true.

Everyone loves the idea of an unexplained mystery and the world will always be full of great stories – you'll read about many of them in this book. Enjoy getting to the truth of the matter but remember, before assuming that something can't be explained, have a good think about what might really be going on.

The puzzle might have a solution, so ask questions, keep an open mind and you might just be the one to solve it . . .

# FLYING IN THE FACE OF DANGER

Two pilots are lost without a trace.
Will we ever know what happened to them?

## AMELIA EARHART

On 2 July 1937, in the city of Lae, Papua New Guinea, Amelia Earhart set off on the trickiest leg of her round-the-world flight. If she made it, she would become the first woman ever to fly around the world. With her, in a tiny Lockheed Electra plane, was navigator Fred Noonan. Four thousand kilometres of Pacific Ocean lay between them and their destination: Howland Island, a speck of land just a few kilometres across.

Four hours in, Amelia sent radio messages to the coastguard. She was close to Howland Island and all was well. But then she was never heard from again. What happened?

Amelia was running out of fuel, the weather was poor, and perhaps she couldn't locate the tiny island. Yet a huge air and sea search was launched and found no trace of her or her plane. Even modern-day searches using high-tech sonar and deep-sea robots have had no success.

What's more, 550 kilometres south of Howland lies the deserted Nikumaroro Island. In 1940, an expedition here discovered tools that appeared to come from a plane, the remains of a woman's shoe, some make-up from the 1930s, and even human bones! Had Amelia flown wildly off course, landed on a different island and set up camp?

When scientists examined the bones in 1940, they said they came from a man. But, 60 years later, scientists changed their minds. The bones belonged to a woman! Now, to complicate things further, the bones have disappeared, so they can't be tested again. The mystery remains ...

## FREDERICK VALENTICH

Young Australian Frederick Valentich was desperate to become a professional pilot. One evening in October 1978, he set off on a solo training flight, flying from Melbourne to King Island in Tasmania.

Just minutes after take-off, he sent a radio message to air traffic control saying he was being followed by something flying about 300 metres above him. There was something odd about the way it flew – it was shiny, and he could see four bright lights on it.

Air traffic control asked Frederick to identify the aircraft. His response was chilling: "It isn't an aircraft." Then they heard awful metal scraping sounds over the radio before it went dead. Frederick was never seen again, and no sign of his plane was ever found.

That same evening, close to the path Frederick's plane took, Roy Manifold was taking pictures of an amazing sunset. Some people claim that one of his photographs might explain what happened. It appears to show an unidentified flying object (UFO) bursting out of the sea into the sky. And that night there were other reports of a UFO with green lights zigzagging across the sky. Had Frederick been abducted by aliens?

Or could there be a simpler explanation? Frederick had found training to be a pilot very difficult. He had failed some flying exams and had little experience of flying at night. It's possible he became disorientated and crashed. But what about the four bright lights? On a clear evening it's not uncommon to see stars and planets shining. Perhaps the lights Frederick saw were Venus, Mars and Mercury, along with Antares, one of the brightest stars in the sky. We may never know the truth for sure.

# LOST AT SEA

These cases might seem obvious, but look closely . . .
Something doesn't quite add up.

## THE FLANNAN ISLES MYSTERY

The Flannan Isles lie in the North Atlantic Ocean, just north-west of the Scottish mainland. No one lives there, but in the early 1800s, three men were working on the island. James Ducat, Thomas Marshall and Donald McArthur were in charge of running the newly built lighthouse, keeping ships safe as they sailed the ferocious seas nearby.

On 26 December 1900, the *Hesperus* sailed to the islands with supplies. However, the crew were surprised to see the lighthouse lamp was not lit. The captain blasted his foghorn and fired a flare, but there was no response. What were the lighthouse keepers doing?

A small team from the *Hesperus* landed on the island. Inside the lighthouse, the beds were unmade and the fire hadn't been lit for days. Most mysteriously, two sets of wet-weather gear were missing, but a third set was still on its hook.

THE LIGHTHOUSE KEEPERS WERE NOWHERE TO BE FOUND.

Search parties combed every inch of the islands. An iron railing was discovered ripped from its foundations. Was it evidence a great wave had hit the island? Perhaps this had swept the men into the sea?

Except . . . the broken railing was 25 metres above sea level. No wave that high had ever been recorded here. And if such a great storm was blowing, why was one set of waterproofs still hanging on its peg?

# THE MISSING MOVIE QUEEN

In the early 1900s, the English actress Marie Empress was known as the 'most beautiful woman in pictures'. She'd moved to America to make her name in Hollywood, where the very first movies were being made.

On 16 October 1919, after visiting the UK, Marie boarded the steam ship *Orduña* to sail back to New York. But when the liner arrived in the US 11 days later, Marie was not on board.

The ship was searched. Marie's cabin was locked from the inside, but once it was opened there was no sign of the movie star. A dinner that had been brought to her cabin had been left uneaten and her bed hadn't been slept in. The cabin window was only 30 centimetres wide – far too narrow to squeeze through.

THERE WAS NO SIGN OF THE MOVIE STAR.

All the passengers on the *Orduña* knew the famous film star, so it would have been almost impossible for her to walk about the busy ship without being noticed. No one at all had seen her on the final evening of the voyage.

In her cabin, investigators found a copy of a message she had sent from the ship to a hotel, booking a room for her arrival. Clearly, she had planned to arrive in New York. Strangely, the public didn't seem too concerned about the missing actress. When news spread that Marie had vanished, people thought it was a publicity stunt; they were sure the actor would turn up at a fancy New York party to surprise everyone. But that didn't happen. Marie's suitcases were never collected from the ship and she was never seen again. The world was left to wonder exactly what had happened on that trip across the Atlantic...

# FACT OR FICTION?

They make great stories, but is there any truth in these tales?

## DRACULA

In 1897, the Irish writer Bram Stoker published what is possibly the most famous horror story ever – *Dracula*. It's also one of the most terrifying! He came up with Count Dracula, Prince of the Undead, a chilling vampire with sharp white fangs who stalks the land at night, hunting for humans in order to suck their blood. But did you know there was once a real-life bloodthirsty Dracula?

He was the 15th-century prince of Wallachia, in Transylvania, Romania. His real name was Vlad III. His father ran a secret society, the Order of the Dragon, and was known as Dracul, the Transylvanian word for *dragon*. So Vlad III became 'son of Dracul', or Dracula. There's no record of Vlad ever sucking blood, but he certainly saw a lot of it. He impaled his enemies on sharpened stakes, stuck them in the ground and left the bodies there to rot. People called him Vlad the Impaler!

But the most mysterious thing about the connection between Vlad and Dracula? About 120 years ago, when researchers dug up Vlad's grave to study his remains, no body was found. So was Vlad actually Prince of the Undead? And might he still be walking among us today?

A VAMPIRE WITH SHARP WHITE FANGS WHO STALKS THE LAND AT NIGHT.

## POPE JOAN

The head of the Roman Catholic Church, the largest church in the world, is the Bishop of Rome, also known as the Pope. The very first pope, almost 2,000 years ago, was St Peter, and every one of the popes since has been a man. Except . . . hundreds of years ago, people whispered stories of Pope Joan – a female pope! She was born sometime in the 800s and was desperate to be educated. Back then, the best place to learn was through the church so she pretended to be a monk, dressed in flowing robes, and rose through the church's ranks until, in 855, she was made Pope.

For two years, her disguise remained a great success until, with dreadful timing, during a procession around Rome, she doubled up in pain. What could the matter be? To the crowd's horror, Pope Joan gave birth on the street . . . which rather gave the game away.

Could this story really be true? A thousand years ago, women had almost no freedom and pretending to be a man might have been the only way to get an education. The problem is, Joan is only ever mentioned in the records hundreds of years after she lived, which makes historians suspicious.

## KING ARTHUR

To the English, King Arthur is a national hero. Brave and chivalrous, he rid the country of deadly foes with his band of followers, the Knights of the Round Table. But did he really exist?

It is thought that a Briton called Arthur did lead a legion of warriors against invaders in the 400s or 500s. No one wrote about him at the time, but a few hundred years later, he started appearing in the history books. Then, in the 1100s, Arthur's legend really took off.

Historian Geoffrey of Monmouth added characters to the story, like Arthur's magician friend, Merlin, and mythical elements such as the sword in the stone. Other writers developed the story further – Arthur's followers became the Knights of the Round Table, their base was Camelot, and they fought dragons, giants and other foul fiends. Before long, it became a fantastical story.

So although it's likely a warrior named Arthur did exist, it's impossible to know how much of the story is true.

# VANISHING VILLAGE

Groups of people don't just disappear . . . or do they?

## THE LOST COLONY OF ROANOKE

In 1587, over 100 men, women and children sailed from England to Roanoke Island – a speck of land off the modern-day US state of North Carolina. They wanted to build the first English settlement in the Americas. It was a difficult journey into the unknown and survival was a struggle. In fact, life was so tough that the leader of the village, John White, decided to return to England after a few weeks for vital supplies.

It took John three years to return to Roanoke, and when he did, he found the entire village had vanished. It looked like John's family and friends had packed up their belongings and left in an orderly manner. But where had they gone without telling him?

THE ENTIRE VILLAGE HAD VANISHED WITHOUT A TRACE.

The only clue was a single word carved on to a tree: CROATOAN. This was the name of a nearby island and the group of Native Americans who lived there. Had the settlers gone to the island to seek help? White set sail to find out but a terrible storm forced him to abandon the journey and return to England.

Over the years, many explorers and archaeologists went to the island to look for evidence. Had the English settlers lived alongside the Croatoans? To this day, no one has been able to work out what really did happen to the settlers on Roanoke Island over 400 years ago.

# GHOST SHIPS

The ocean can be a bewildering place. It's all too easy to find yourself sailing into trouble.

## THE MARY CELESTE

On 7 November 1872, the *Mary Celeste* set off from New York in the USA. Built 10 years earlier, she had a history of accidents and had become known as an unlucky ship. Now she was on her way to Genoa in Italy, with Captain Benjamin Spooner Briggs, his wife, their two-year-old daughter and seven crew members on board.

One month into the voyage, sailors on another ship, *Dei Gratia*, spotted the *Mary Celeste*. She was still more than 1,500 kilometres from Europe and drifting unpredictably. Some crew from the *Dei Gratia* climbed aboard the *Mary Celeste* to investigate, and what they discovered can still not be explained today …

## THERE WAS NOBODY ON BOARD.

A single lifeboat had been launched and some navigational equipment was missing. But while the ship was a little weather-beaten, she was perfectly seaworthy. There was no sign of fighting or of fire breaking out. Some stories even claim there were steaming mugs of tea and half-eaten breakfasts still on the table. Captain Briggs, his family and the crew were never seen again.

So why was the ship abandoned? There have been all kinds of suggestions. Pirates from north Africa could have attacked, a great storm might have hit them, and some claim an underwater earthquake might have scared them into abandoning ship. Some people even believe the crew of the *Dei Gratia* killed everyone on board.

Ultimately, though, there was never any evidence to support these theories, so we may never find out exactly what happened …

## THE FLYING DUTCHMAN

In 1881, Prince George of Wales was serving on a Royal Navy ship off the coast of Australia when he spotted something extraordinary. Out of the gloom, a ghostly ship appeared, glowing red.

In 1939, dozens of people on a beach in Cape Town, South Africa, saw a ship sailing directly for the shore, only for it to vanish moments before it ploughed into the sand.

These are just two of many strange sightings. The ship, named the *Flying Dutchman*, is said to sail the oceans for the rest of time. And that's not all. Once the ship has been spotted by another ship's crew, legend has it disaster will follow.

But who's on board? The captain is said to be Hendrick Vanderdecken, a Dutchman who, sometime in the 1600s, was taking silks and spices from Indonesia to Holland. Approaching the Cape of Good Hope at the southern tip of Africa, the ship hit a mighty storm. The crew pleaded with their captain to turn the ship round, but Vanderdecken refused. Worse, he promised that they would make it around the Cape, even if it meant they had to sail forever. And with this curse …

THE FLYING DUTCHMAN AND ITS CREW WERE DOOMED FOR ALL ETERNITY!

But could there be another explanation? The mind can play tricks on people who spend a lot of time at sea. Unusual atmospheric conditions, moisture in the air and changing temperatures can lead to strange illusions known as mirages. Ships that are almost out of sight can appear weirdly close and, sometimes, they can even seem to float above the water. Throw in some sailors' superstition, and it's the perfect recipe for a ghostly tale.

# VISITORS FROM OUTER SPACE

## UFOs aren't so unusual . . . So does that mean aliens are heading our way?

UFO stands for Unidentified Flying Object. They might appear as balls of light, spinning saucers or unusual cigar-shaped craft, but what links all UFOs is that they can't be explained by anything made by humans. Many people believe these strange objects could be alien spaceships and the US government has spent millions of dollars investigating them over the years.

Are aliens real? No one knows for sure, but here are some mysterious UFO sightings so you can make up your own mind!

### THE JAPAN AIRLINES INCIDENT

In 1986, pilots on a Japan Airlines flight over Alaska, USA, were startled to see two UFOs in the night sky. It was difficult to make out the shapes in the darkness, but both had huge, glowing rocket thrusters that were so powerful the pilots could feel the heat on their faces. After flying together for 10 minutes, the two UFOs dipped out of sight, only to be replaced by something even more extraordinary: a flying machine, which pilot, Captain Terauchi, described as "twice the size of an aircraft carrier". But by the time military aircraft arrived, the flying objects had disappeared.

### THE TRANS-EN-PROVENCE INCIDENT

In 1981, Renato Nicolai was working on his farm in the south of France when he saw something peculiar. A flying machine, shaped like two saucers placed back to back and the size of a small car, hovered above the ground just metres away. It stayed there for 30 seconds before rising above the trees and flying off. Immediately, Renato ran to where the flying saucer had been. There was nothing there except a patch of burnt black grass. Scientific analysis revealed traces of unusual chemicals and evidence that the grass had been heated to a scorching 300°C!

## THE USS NIMITZ INCIDENT

In 2004, US Navy pilot, David Fravor, strapped himself into his fighter jet and took off from the aircraft carrier USS *Nimitz*. He was investigating reports of an unusual aircraft over the sea near San Diego, USA. Minutes into the flight, David spotted a patch of choppy water and headed in for a closer look. Suddenly, a lozenge-shaped flying object appeared out of nowhere. David had never seen anything like it. With no wings and no obvious engine, how had it even got off the ground? Before he could intercept the craft and find out who – or what – was on board, it shot off, at three times the speed of sound.

SUDDENLY, A FLYING OBJECT APPEARED OUT OF NOWHERE.

## THE MANSFIELD HELICOPTER INCIDENT

In 1973, an army helicopter in Ohio, USA, almost crashed into a UFO. The pilot, Major Larry Coyne, saw a red light on the horizon. He thought nothing of it until the light started accelerating directly towards him! Larry desperately tried to land his helicopter, but knew he wasn't going to make it in time. Bracing himself for collision, he was amazed to discover the cigar-shaped object hadn't hit him, but instead, hovered above him. Larry continued to try to land his helicopter, but realised he wasn't going down, but up! His aircraft was being pulled towards the alien craft. Then there was a bump, the helicopter dipped slightly, and the strange craft was gone . . .

# ALIEN ENCOUNTERS – CLOSE UP!

These people don't just claim to have spotted a UFO... They've been on board!

## ROBERT TAYLOR

One morning in November 1979, just outside Edinburgh, Scotland, forester Robert 'Bob' Taylor jumped into his van with his dog Lara and set off for work. He was going on his usual trip to the woods, to check for stray cattle or sheep.

Once in the woods, Lara raced off into the undergrowth as Bob made his way into a clearing. Suddenly, he was hit by a brilliant beam of light. In front of him was a flying saucer as big as an elephant. It was made of grey metal, with propellers round its rim.

Two spiked spheres dropped from the craft on to the grass. They seemed to know Bob was there and rolled towards him. Then a spike on each sphere hooked on to Bob's trouser legs. A foul burning smell surrounded him...

THEN BOB FELT HIMSELF BEING PULLED TOWARDS THE SAUCER.

Bob blacked out. When he woke up, Lara was barking furiously but the visitors had gone. Bob's trousers were torn and covered in mud, he had cuts on his chin and a bad headache. Later, examining the clearing with police, Bob found the grass had been pressed flat as if something heavy had hovered above it. There were also a series of holes pushed into the earth, perhaps made by the spiky spheres.

This part of Scotland has hundreds of UFO sightings every year. But did Bob end up going one step further and actually get taken on board?

## BARNEY AND BETTY HILL

Late one night in September 1961, Barney and Betty Hill were driving through New Hampshire, USA, when they noticed a bright light in the sky. The light got closer and closer and, strangely, seemed to be following them. Soon the pair could make out the outline of a peculiar craft, shaped like a huge pancake. What on Earth was it?

The pancake got lower until it was hovering above the couple's car. Barney hit the brakes and got out to take a closer look. He could see grey figures through the spaceship's windows and a ramp began to extend from the bottom of the craft. Somehow, Barney knew these visitors wanted to take him and Betty. He leaped back into the car to escape, but weird noises surrounded the couple and a tingling shock fizzed through their bodies. Both of them lost consciousness.

Two hours later, the pair woke up on a totally different road. They discovered that their clothes were torn and their shoes were damaged. They were covered in fine pink dust and their car was dotted with strange shiny marks. Neither of them could remember what had happened.

Later on, Barney was hypnotised to see if he could recall anything. He told the hypnotist about being taken on to the spaceship, where human-like beings with large eyes studied him and Betty. They took locks of their hair and nail clippings and peered into their ears and mouths. It was as if the visitors were trying to understand how human bodies worked. Barney remembered communicating with their captors through their minds. When it was time for Barney and Betty to leave, they had their memories erased.

Did these two extraordinary events really happen? Bob Taylor and Barney and Betty Hill all insisted they did.

# ALIEN EVIDENCE

## Are aliens already here?

### WOW!

'SETI' stands for the 'Search for Extra-Terrestrial Intelligence' – in other words, aliens! SETI scientists listen in on the universe to see if they can hear anyone else out there. To help them eavesdrop, scientists use radio telescopes – enormous dishes that can pick up the faintest radio signals from deep space. The universe is a noisy place, because planets and stars also send out natural radio waves, so finding something unusual is tricky. Everything the dishes hear is recorded, so researchers can quickly spot anything odd.

For years, SETI scientists found nothing. Then on 15 August 1977, astronomer Jerry Ehman looked at a page of data from the Big Ear radio telescope in Ohio, USA. He couldn't believe what he was looking at – a radio signal, lasting over a minute, that was 30 times stronger than any other signal SETI projects had ever identified. Jerry was so amazed that he picked up his red pen, circled the data, and scribbled 'WOW!' next to it. Since then, it's always been known as the 'WOW! signal'.

So was it aliens? Even now, no one can be sure. Nothing like it has ever been heard again. All we know is that the universe is so massive that it's likely there is intelligent life out there . . . somewhere.

## ARE ALIENS LIVING IN THE USA?

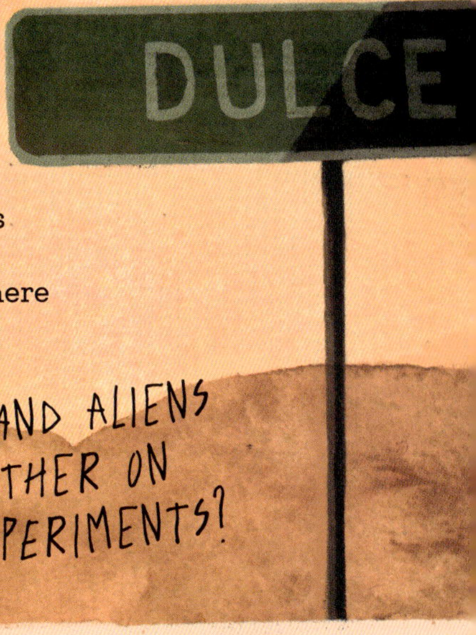


Dulce is a small town in New Mexico, USA. In the 1970s, people started to spot both UFOs and US military helicopters regularly flying overhead. What was going on?

A UFO enthusiast, Paul Bennewitz, believed unusual radio signals were being transmitted from the area. He was convinced the US military were working with aliens in a secret underground complex. Another enthusiast, Phil Schneider, said that he had actually worked there. He described a seven-storey complex built underground where UFOs could land. Here, humans and aliens worked on scientific experiments. Phil even claimed he had lost three fingers when an alien had fired a laser blaster at him!

Is any of this true? Around Dulce, there's no evidence – few roads, no car parks, no doors leading underground, no air vents ... nothing you might expect to see for an underground base. But perhaps that's the point. It's a secret complex, after all!

DID HUMANS AND ALIENS WORK TOGETHER ON SCIENTIFIC EXPERIMENTS?

## DID A FLYING SAUCER CRASH-LAND ON EARTH?

In July 1947, William Brazel found some unusual rubbish on a ranch outside Roswell, New Mexico, USA. Brazel showed the tin foil, wood and rubber strips to an army officer, Major Jesse Marcel, who then investigated the site. The following day the local newspaper's headline announced that a crashed flying saucer had been found!

The US military quickly denied the claim. They said the material was from a high-altitude weather balloon, but people thought they were covering up the facts. UFO believers even claimed that aliens who had died in the crash were found inside the wreckage.

The researchers believed the wreckage and bodies were taken to Area 51, a highly secret US military base in Nevada. Here, it was thought that the flying saucer was investigated by engineers to find out how alien technology worked, while medical experts examined the bodies to help them understand alien biology.

The US military deny that any of this ever happened ...

# LIGHTS IN THE SKY

Most lights have a simple explanation, but every now and then, something puzzling appears.

## LIGHT PILLARS

Light pillars are beams of light that shoot from Earth high into the sky, as if someone is shining a powerful spotlight into the night. You won't see them in a city – there are too many other bright lights – but on clear, cold nights in the countryside, where there are fewer street lights, it can sometimes look as if there's a forest of lights across the sky.

At first, you might think they are caused by something supernatural, or that an alien is lighting up its route to Earth but, in fact, this beautiful natural phenomenon is caused by ice.

When it is cold enough, moisture in the air freezes to form thousands of tiny ice crystals. If the ice crystals are the right shape – with flat sides – they can act like tiny mirrors, reflecting any light below them back down to Earth. When the air is thick with these ice crystals, lots of light is reflected and anyone close by sees a strange pillar towering into the sky.

## THE AURORAS

The Aurora Borealis (Northern Lights) and Aurora Australis (Southern Lights) are beautiful shimmering bands of colour that stretch across the sky in the far north and south of our planet. In ancient mythology these lights were bridges to other worlds. But what are they really?

The lights appear when streams of charged particles from the sun hit our atmosphere. Earth has its own powerful magnetic field – it's why we have a North and South Pole – and the sun's particles are swept towards the poles by this magnetic force. Here, they collide with molecules in our atmosphere and energy is released as light – which we see as the Auroras.

Even though scientists know exactly how these lights are formed, there is something rather magical about seeing these glowing ribbons of reds, greens and blues tangle across the night sky, and it's easy to see why people once believed they were mysterious pathways to the gods.

BALLS OF LIGHT HOVER OVER THE VALLEY, DAY AND NIGHT.

## THE HESSDALEN LIGHTS

Strange things happen in the sky above the village of Hessdalen in Norway. For almost 100 years, people here have noticed balls of light hovering over the valley, day and night. Each ball is as big as a car and appears to float for hours at a time. Some people believe they must be aliens, but can science reveal more?

After years of investigation, there are many theories. One idea is that the whole valley behaves like a giant battery, powerful enough to turn pockets of air into glowing balls of light. It's a bizarre theory based on the kinds of rocks found in the river there. Other researchers believe cosmic rays – tiny, high-energy particles blasted from the sun – might be to blame. Another theory is that natural radiation here creates balls of plasma – a gas so packed full of energy it glows. Experts can't agree about what is causing the lights. Perhaps one day they'll discover they are aliens after all!

# FALLING FROM THE SKY

Rain is the least of your worries.
Imagine getting caught in one of these downpours.

## BLOOD RAIN

For three months in 2001, blood-red rain fell over Kerala in southern India. Though unusual, it wasn't the first time. Throughout history this strange phenomenon has occured more than once. People often believed it was a sign that something dreadful was about to happen, so people in Kerala became worried.

Scientists have examined blood rain before . . . and found no blood. They discovered that specks of red dust turned the raindrops red. Sandstorms, in places like the Sahara Desert in Africa, whip dust high into the atmosphere, where eventually it gets mixed into clouds and falls as red-coloured rain.

But scientists studying the blood rain in Kerala were in for a big shock. While it wasn't blood, it wasn't dust either! Worse, they found something alive in the rain, something that didn't look like anything they'd seen before.

What was going on? Just before the rain in Kerala began, space scientists had reported a mysterious alien object exploding in our upper atmosphere. Could the two things be connected? Was this blood rain an alien attack?

When researchers took a closer look, they discovered the red rain contained lichen spores, a kind of fungus that grows on trees. And they found the same lichen on trees in Kerala. So . . . it probably wasn't an alien invasion. But how exactly did the lichen spores get up into the clouds? Scientists haven't answered that one yet . . .

## JELLY RAIN

Imagine waking up in the morning and finding weird jelly all over the garden. That's exactly what happened to people living in Penland, Scotland, in 2009. The strange, white, wobbly blobs were found across fields and even in trees. What was it? And where had it come from?

People used to believe jelly fell to Earth when space rocks hit our planet's atmosphere. They called it star jelly. But, even today, we're no closer to discovering what it really is. Scientists doubt it comes from outer space, but think it might be the remains of frogs or frogspawn, a kind of slime mould or something called a bryozoan – tiny water creatures that can form great jelly-like groups. Any of these theories might be true, but it still doesn't explain why it fell from the sky . . .

## FISH FROM THE SKY

In 1855, in Yoro, a small town in Honduras, people were poor and hungry. A priest, Father José Manuel Subirana, prayed for some kind of miracle to provide food. After three days, a huge storm hit the town. When the rains cleared, scattered across the ground were hundreds of silver fish. Dinner!

Every year for the past 100 years, the people of Yoro have celebrated the Rain of Fish, and fish still occasionally appear flipping and flapping on the streets after some rainstorms. And Yoro isn't alone. There are reports of fish from the sky throughout history, from ancient Greece to Australia.

So is it a miracle? Most experts think it's not, but there aren't many scientific theories that can explain this weird phenomenon. Some believe that small whirlwinds form over nearby lakes and drag water, and fish, into the air. Eventually, what goes up, must come down. Or perhaps the fish haven't come from the sky at all? Underground rivers that run in caves beneath Yoro sometimes flood after heavy rainfall, which might push the fish to the surface. But if the experts' theories are right, wouldn't the streets be littered with all kinds of river creatures, not just silver fish?

SCATTERED ACROSS THE GROUND WERE HUNDREDS OF SILVER FISH.

# EARTH'S UNEXPLAINED AREAS

Some claim parts of our planet have strange energies . . .

## THE MAPIMÍ SILENT ZONE

On 11 July 1970, a seven-ton, five-storey-high rocket blasted off from a military base in Utah, USA. It was on a test flight, heading for an air force base in New Mexico. However, something went wrong with its navigation system and it didn't make it to the landing site. It crashed close to the town of Chihuahua, in the Mapimí Desert, Mexico.

Desperate for the missile not to fall into the wrong hands, the US government quickly sent teams to look for it. Finding the rogue rocket was tricky, though. Once in Mapimí, the teams found that none of their radios and walkie-talkies would work. After weeks of searching, the rocket was finally spotted and recovered. The US military left, but the mystery of the radios remained.

The missile had landed in the heart of an area known as *la Zona del Silencio* – the Silent Zone. It's said that electronic equipment doesn't work here . . . and perhaps that's why the American missile crashed in the first place. Other weird things happen here too. Animals and plants are said to grow much bigger than normal, magnetic compasses don't work, the place is littered with meteorites, and reports of UFOs are common. Many people even believe they've met aliens here. What could be going on?

Some people believe the ground gives off a strange 'earth energy', thanks to unusual minerals in the soil. They can't explain what this energy is or how it affects things, but they say it's a powerful force. Others have a different opinion. They think the whole story has been made up to encourage tourists to visit the site to help local businesses make money.

Unexplained earth energy or extra-terrestrial tourist trap? The only way to find out? Head there yourself!

## THE BERMUDA TRIANGLE

On 5 December 1945, five military planes took off on a training flight from their base in Florida, USA. Once they were over the ocean, things very quickly went wrong. Something odd started happening to the cockpit dials and controls, so the pilots couldn't tell where they were or how high they were flying. They became confused and didn't know which way they needed to fly to get back.

As the planes began to run low on fuel, the pilots radioed for help. They needed to find solid ground quickly so they could land their aircraft. A rescue plane set out to look for them, but it too vanished.

NONE OF THE PLANES OR THE 27 CREW WERE EVER FOUND.

This is just one of many tragic events that have happened in the Bermuda Triangle, a stretch of sea between Bermuda, the Florida coast and Puerto Rico, that is steeped in myth and mystery. Over the years, hundreds of ships and planes have disappeared in the triangle. The question is, why?

There are all kinds of weird theories. Supernatural forces, magnetic energies or cracks in the seabed – where underwater volcanoes belch out hot flammable gases.

But researchers believe they finally have the answer. Lots of planes and ships do run into difficulties in the Bermuda Triangle . . . but no more than is expected. It's a dangerous area of the world where storms can blow up very quickly. However, more importantly, it's also a very busy region. If a lot of planes and ships pass through the triangle, it makes sense that the number of them that get into trouble will be higher too!

# BIZARRE BOULDERS

Nothing's set in stone when it comes to these mysterious rocks.

## SAILING STONES

In 1915, gold-hunter Joseph Crook was hoping to make his fortune in Nevada, USA. He was exploring a dry lake bed in Death Valley when he spotted something extraordinary. Long tracks were scraped into the dirt. They appeared to have come from stones moving across the lake bed. But there were no footprints . . .

THE ROCKS MUST HAVE MOVED BY THEMSELVES.

Some of the rocks were so huge, they couldn't have been blown by the wind. Some of the tracks were straight, some were curved, and some even had sharp angles in them. What was going on?

For years, people had no idea. Then, in the 1970s, a team of geologists gave 30 stones names and started to record their movements. In the first 12 months, 10 stones moved. Mary-Ann travelled 65 metres; Nancy, the smallest stone, clocked up an impressive 201 metres; and one stone, Karen, actually disappeared!

Decades later, motion-sensitive cameras were used to track the rocks. The cameras revealed that in winter, pools of water froze overnight and melted in the morning. Huge sheets of ice, floating in the puddles, were blown by the wind and bulldozed some of the rocks, driving them through the wet mud. But although that seems to be how the smaller rocks are moving, no one has ever seen one of the bigger rocks budge an inch . . .

## SHIFTING SANDS

In the Olduvai Gorge in Tanzania, Africa, there are two large black sand dunes. Not only do they look out of place because they're much darker than the nearby soil – they do something very odd.

These great, crescent-shaped mounds actually move, creeping over 10 metres a year! In fact, scientists believe they have been roaming across the savannah for around three million years. And what's even weirder is that the sand in these dunes sticks together. If a handful is thrown up into the air, it won't scatter in the wind. Instead, the strange black particles clump together and fall back down to Earth.

The local people, the Maasai, believe the sands are sacred and come from the nearby Ol Doinyo Lengai mountain, or Mountain of God. But there is another explanation. It's been discovered that these dunes are made of volcanic ash that is packed with magnetic iron. When it's blown by the wind, the magnetic attraction means the dunes never break up. Instead they move grain by grain, inch by inch, wandering the plains together for evermore . . .

## RINGING ROCKS

The town of Upper Black Eddy in Pennsylvania, USA, is known for its rock music. In a forest clearing, known as Ringing Rocks Park, lie thousands of mysterious musical rocks. They're all different shapes and sizes, and if one is gently struck with a hammer, it will ring clearly like a bell.

The rocks are made of a material known as diabase and while some diabase rocks found in other places around the world sing, many more don't. In fact, only around a third of the Black Eddy rocks actually ring beautifully. So what's so special about these?

Some people believe the musical chimes are down to supernatural forces. They claim the lack of plants and animals living around the rocks suggests something creepy is going on, but others argue that most wildlife would struggle to live in a patch of land covered in boulders anyway.

Geologists think that the most likely explanation is probably something to do with how these rocks were originally formed deep inside the Earth but, as yet, it's a musical mystery that remains unsolved . . .

# WEIRD WATERS

Watch out! You could find yourself in deep water.

## MYSTERIOUS DESERT LAKES

In Inner Mongolia, in the north of China, lies the huge Badain Jaran Desert. It's home to some of the biggest sand dunes in the world, which are taller than New York's Empire State Building. Nestled between these giant dunes, in the middle of the hot dry desert, are over 100 lakes. It's no wonder the Mongolians call this place 'Mysterious Lakes'.

WHAT ARE LAKES DOING IN THE MIDDLE OF THE DESERT?

Some researchers suspect they're made up of water from cracks and pores in rocks under the desert floor, which has possibly been there for thousands of years. Others believe the water comes from streams that start hundreds of kilometres away in the mountains that surround the desert. Up here in the high snowy peaks, when ice melts, the resulting water seeps into the earth and eventually trickles into the desert.

But why doesn't the water just bleed away into the hot dry sand? Some people think it's because the sand here is so fine. When it gets wet, it clumps together to form a gluey plug. This stops the rest of the water draining away and traps it in these pools. However these lakes came to exist, they truly are a bizarre sight.

## BLOOD FALLS

On the edge of Antarctica, what looks like a waterfall of blood tumbles into a frozen lake. Over 30 metres high, this 'blood fall' has been a mystery ever since it was first discovered over 100 years ago. Now scientists believe they know what is going on . . .

The blood-red ice is part of a slow-moving column of frozen water called the Taylor Glacier that begins life as a sunken lake of icy water 400 metres underground. It takes 1.5 million years to creep to the surface. However, the mystery is that the glacier looks just like any other. The ice only turns blood-red when it reaches the surface.

While there's no blood in the ice, it's something found in blood that's turning the ice red – iron. This iron is scraped off iron-rich rocks by the glacier deep underground. Then it is slowly brought to the surface where it hits oxygen, found in air, for the first time. Here, it does what iron does in air – it rusts – and, in doing so, it turns the ice blood-red.

## THE MILKSHAKE LAKE

On a tiny island off south-west Australia is an extraordinary lake. Just metres from the deep blue ocean, surrounded by a ring of trees, is a lake so pink it looks like strawberry milkshake. And while it most definitely is water, scientists haven't quite agreed on what gives it such an unusual colour.

The lake was written about in 1802 by Matthew Flinders, an English navigator who studied and drew maps of the Australian coast. He named it Lake Hillier, after a friend of his on the same voyage.

But why is it pink? Scientists agree that it's down to tiny microbes – but disagree about exactly which ones. Some believe it's because of a plant-like algae called Dunaliella salina. Others point to another kind of organism known as archaea, which is the oldest form of life ever discovered. These single-cell microbes have been around for 3.5 billion years and were probably the first living things to exist on our planet. Both these tiny organisms produce things called carotenoids – they are what give carrots, peppers and tomatoes their bright colours. And, it would appear, sometimes lakes too!

# STRANGE CIRCLES

These remarkable rings have got researchers scratching their heads.

## DESERT FAIRY CIRCLES

The Namib Desert in Namibia is peppered with peculiar 'fairy circles'. While most of the desert floor is covered in shrubs and grasses, hardy plants that can cope with the tough conditions, there are also thousands of circles in which nothing – absolutely nothing – grows at all. When seen from above, it looks like the desert has come out in a rash.

The people that live here, the Himba, say that the circles aren't made by fairies at all, but are the footprints of the god Mukuru. Another local myth tells of a dragon that lives below the desert, whose poisonous breath kills the plants growing above.

But is there a more likely explanation? Researchers have discovered a colony of termites living below each circle. These ant-like creatures chew through any plant roots in their way, leaving a barren patch of earth on top. However, termite colonies don't get on and continually fight with each other, creating zones between the colonies where no termites live. Here, in this termite 'no-man's land', plants flourish, creating the extraordinary fairy circles.

## ICE CIRCLES FROM SPACE

In 2009, astronauts on the International Space Station spotted something curious in one of the deepest and oldest lakes in the world, Lake Baikal in Siberia, Russia. It's so cold there that ice over a metre thick can form on the lake's surface, but when astronauts peered down from space, they noticed huge rings carved into the ice. They were over three kilometres wide – what giant could have created these?

Legend has it that a water dragon lives beneath the ice. It created the lake by swinging its huge tail, cracking open the earth. So are a dragon's flames creating the circles? Scientists drilled through the ice and sent cameras to the bottom of the lake to explore. Here, they discovered it's not a dragon breathing fire but the Earth! Scattered across the lake bed are dozens of mini-volcanoes that belch out hot gases from deep within the planet.

These gases warm the water and incredibly strong underwater currents develop as the hot water rises and cold water falls, eventually generating giant, spinning vortices (whirlpools) of warm water. It's these whirlpools that melt huge circles in the ice above them, which can be seen from space.

## CROP SHOCK?

In 1978, odd things started happening in farmland across the south of England. Bizarre circular patterns of flattened crops appeared in fields overnight.

### WHAT WAS CAUSING THESE STRANGE CROP CIRCLES?

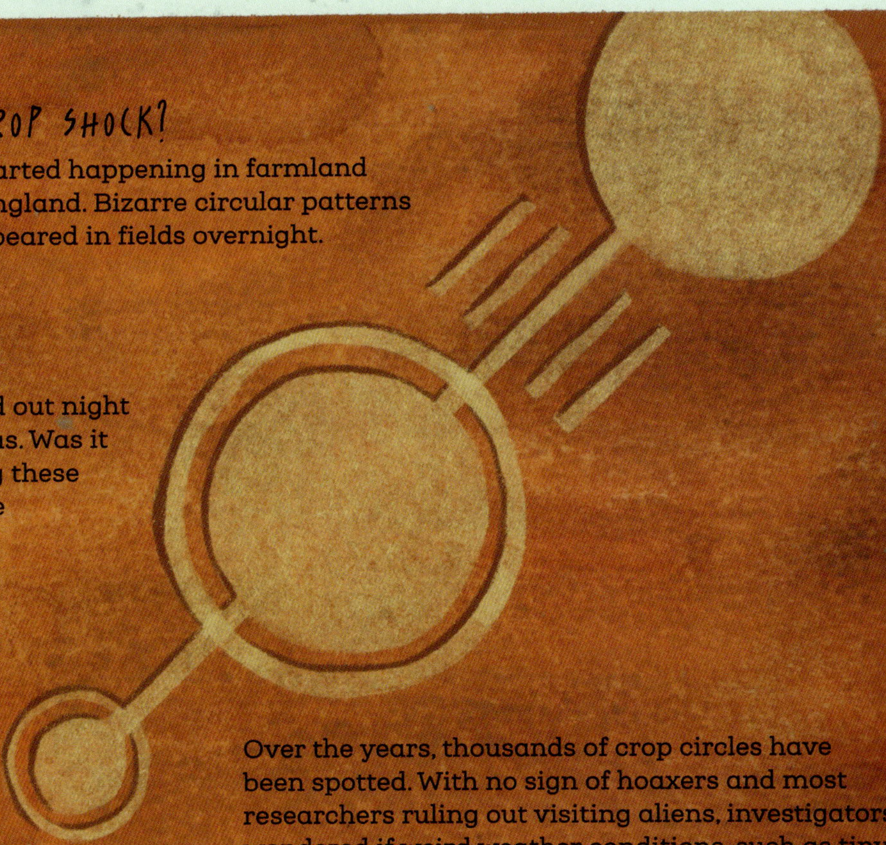

Investigators, known as 'cerealogists', camped out night after night or set up motion-sensitive cameras. Was it some unknown natural phenomenon causing these crop circles? Or, more intriguingly, were these landing sites for flying saucers?

Over the years, thousands of crop circles have been spotted. With no sign of hoaxers and most researchers ruling out visiting aliens, investigators wondered if weird weather conditions, such as tiny whirlwinds, might be to blame.

Then, 20 years after the first circles appeared, the mystery was solved when two farmers, Doug Bower and David Chorley, confessed all. They had used simple technology – ropes and planks of wood – to flatten the crops to create the first circles. Others, who had guessed that pranksters were behind the circles, copied Doug and David and so the phenomenon spread.

# FISHY TALES?

There are plenty of fish in the sea, but there might be other – rather bigger – things there too!

Oceans are deep, dark, dangerous places, so it's no surprise there have been tales of sea monsters for as long as we've been sailing ships across the waters. New fish species are being discovered all the time, so perhaps we shouldn't be surprised if some of the terrifying creatures claimed to have been encountered over the centuries are, in fact, real.

## HERE BE MONSTERS!

Ancient maps from medieval times didn't only tell you where different countries were, they also revealed what sailors thought lay below the waves. Dangerous parts of the oceans were marked with warnings. It was believed for hundreds of years that every kind of animal on land, had its equivalent at sea. There were sea dogs, sea lions . . . and even sea pigs!

But there were more extraordinary animals on these maps too, like the ichthyocentaur, a horrifying mix of serpent, human and horse, or whale-like monsters with great tusks, and even deadly sirens – mermaids that could bewitch sailors and send them to a watery grave with their singing. And then there was the kraken.

THE KRAKEN WAS ONE OF THE MOST FEARED SEA CREATURES EVER.

The kraken was a giant squid big enough to wrap itself around a ship and haul it underwater. Sightings of this terrible beast were especially common in the waters around Scandinavian countries. There are many tales of sailors heading to the safety of an island, only to discover it was a kraken lying in wait.

These ancient stories are hard to believe now. Tales grow taller over time and become the stuff of myth and legend. Are there more recent, reliable sightings of monsters? Well, yes! Plenty.

## SUBMARINE SIGHTING

During the First World War, German U-boat UB-85 was on patrol one evening off the British coast, on the lookout for enemy ships. As the submarine surfaced, the crew felt a huge thud as something below the water struck the vessel. It's claimed the captain, Günter Krech, watched in alarm as a terrifying sea monster emerged from the water and climbed on to his submarine. The creature had great big eyes in a small horny skull, and its teeth glistened in the moonlight.

The submarine began to slip back beneath the waves under the weight of the watery horror, so Günter ordered his crew to open fire. Eventually, the monster slithered back into the inky blackness. The damage left UB-85 unable to move. When a British Royal Navy ship, HMS *Coreopsis II*, arrived the next morning, the German crew were relieved to surrender and be rescued.

SOMETHING BELOW THE WATER STRUCK THE VESSEL.

## ATLANTIC ODYSSEY

Fifty years later, it was British soldiers who came across a monster from the deep. Captain John Ridgeway and Sergeant Chay Blyth were attempting to cross the Atlantic Ocean in a rowing boat in the summer of 1966.

Late one night in the middle of the crossing, John noticed the water churned up close to their boat and believed he had spotted something writhing and twisting below the surface. Whatever it was, it was over 10 metres long and glowed in the dark. It seemed to be following the men, swimming around and underneath their boat. John was frozen with fear, expecting the vessel to flip over. If it did, they would both surely die. Thankfully, the mysterious creature eventually swam away, leaving the pair to wonder what it had been.

# THE LOCH NESS MONSTER

Monsters don't only live in the ocean. Dip your toe in this Scottish loch and you might get a shock.

THOUSANDS OF TOURISTS VISIT SCOTLAND EACH YEAR HOPING TO CATCH SIGHT OF HER.

The most famous aquatic monster is the Loch Ness monster which is said to live in the heart of Scotland. It's a place of massive mountains and deep dark lakes. It's thick with myth and mystery, with tales of monsters, sprites and shadowy spirits. But while most people understand these are just stories, somehow 'Nessie' is different.

Some people have devoted their whole lives to tracking her down. But is she real, or just another myth? Loch Ness is 36 kilometres long and over 200 metres deep, certainly big enough to hold a monster.

Many claim to have seen her. They describe a huge water beast with a long tail and neck, a plump body and four big flippers. To experts, the description sounds like something familiar, a huge marine reptile called a plesiosaur. There's just one problem. Plesiosaurs died out over 65 million years ago.

### JUST A STORY?

Evidence for the Loch Ness monster is thin on the ground. Plesiosaurs died out with the dinosaurs, so could the Loch Ness monster – and other ancient beasts – really have survived? Though it seems incredible, it's not impossible. Crocodiles, sharks and horseshoe crabs all lived at the time of the dinosaurs and they've survived, generation after generation, for millions of years. The difference is they've not been hidden away for all that time, like Nessie. However, even this has happened before.

In 1938, a fish called a coelacanth was discovered. We know that this fish was around at the same time as the dinosaurs because we've found fossils – and for years experts believed it was extinct because it had never been seen alive. That was until one popped up in a fisherman's net off the coast of South Africa. It had been hiding from humans for almost 70 million years! So if the coelacanth can survive out of sight, perhaps Nessie could too.

# WILD THINGS!

If you go down to the woods today . . . you might get a big surprise.

## BIGFOOT

In the forests of north-west America, something unusual lurks among the trees. It walks upright on two legs like a human, but is much bigger and is covered in thick dark hair. The only apes in North America are usually kept in zoos, so what could it possibly be?

For over 200 years, Native Americans have told tales of a wild man that lives in the woods. While some stories describe a child-snatching monster, others tell of a harmless creature that keeps itself to itself. They called this monster Sasquatch. Today we know it as Bigfoot.

But what's the evidence that Bigfoot is real? Massive footprints twice the size of a human's have been sighted, and some believe tufts of fur found on bushes and brambles belong to the beast. Many people believe they've actually spotted the creature in the wild and a handful have even caught it on camera. Famously, in 1967, two friends in Bluff Creek, California, filmed a hairy man-shaped beast striding alongside the river. Was this Bigfoot? Or somebody in a gorilla suit?

## THE YETI

The Yeti, or Abominable Snowman, is another ape-like beast, but this one lives in the snowy peaks of the Himalayas, in Asia. The local people have legends and folk tales that talk of a 'glacier creature' but it was only in the early 1900s, when explorers from the USA and Europe arrived, that stories of the Yeti began to spread.

Giant footprints had been found in the snow, and some explorers claimed to have seen the creature for themselves. In 1942, one man described two creatures that he believed were yetis. He said "their heads were squarish ... the arms were long and the wrists reach the level of the knees". Could it be true? The Himalayas are so wild and unexplored, perhaps undiscovered creatures are still waiting to be found there ...

## THE YOWIE

In the remote mountains around Australia's Gold Coast lives the Yowie, a three-metre-tall creature with big feet and an ape-like face. The Aboriginal people have always told stories of the Yowie and sightings are still happening today. In 2019, a delivery driver, known only as Gary, said he stopped his truck on a deserted forest road only for a 'towering beast' to leap out and bash his bonnet before disappearing into the bush.

## COULD THIS HAVE BEEN A REAL-LIFE SIGHTING?

Regions all around the world seem to have their own wild-man tales. Are they simply creepy stories? Or are they real? If these creatures do exist, why is there not more evidence? Surely there's not just one Bigfoot, or one Yeti ... they must belong to families or a group. So where are they? And when almost everyone now carries a mobile-phone camera around with them, why are even the best images of these creatures still blurry and unclear?

And yet ... discoveries of new creatures do still happen. Previously unheard of by Europeans, unfamiliar animal species like the mountain gorilla or Komodo dragon only became widely known in the early 1900s. Incredibly, a race of humans the size of four-year-olds, *Homo-floresiensis*, was discovered recently too. They lived 12,000 years ago which is a blink of an eye in human history. So perhaps it's not too far-fetched to think these other creatures really are out there ...

# KILLER CATS AND FISH-GOATS!

Keep your wits about you . . .
Strange animals lurk after dark.

## THE BEAST OF BODMIN MOOR

Bodmin Moor in the south-west of England is a place of windswept moorland, rocky outcrops and deep swirling rivers. It's full of wildlife, but there's one animal that's said to stalk the land and strikes terror into the hearts of all who have seen it – the Beast of Bodmin Moor.

THE MOORLAND WAS COVERED WITH HUGE PAWPRINTS.

It was first spotted in the 1970s and hundreds of people have seen it since. Over the years, possible proof of its existence has also been produced, including pawprints and blurry photos that suggest it looks a bit like a panther. Farmers have also blamed the beast for mysterious attacks on their animals.

In 1995, a skull with two huge fangs was found in a river on the moor. Was this the skull of the beast? Experts identified it as a leopard skull, but they also discovered something else. Inside the skull was the tiny egg case of a cockroach. They knew cockroaches don't live on Bodmin Moor, so this leopard must have died somewhere else. In other words, the skull was a hoax.

There are still reports of a beast roaming the moor to this day. So what could it be? Some people believe that since a nearby zoo closed down in 1978, some of its pumas escaped and found their way to the wilds of Bodmin. Is it true? No one knows, but perhaps it's wise not to be out on the moor too late at night . . .

## "FISHY MAN-GOAT TERRIFIES COUPLES PARKED AT LAKE WORTH"

It's a crazy headline . . . but true. Back in the summer of 1969, in the Fort Worth Nature Centre in Texas, USA, visitors were scared witless by a two-metre-tall creature covered in both fish scales and fur, with a long neck and the horned head of a goat. There were reports of it attacking sheep and picking up the wheel of a car and throwing it like a Frisbee.

Locals had long told tales of a monster in the area, but there had never been any sightings. But that summer the Fort Worth Monster made its first appearance, leading to stories in the newspapers. Visitors flocked to the park, hoping to catch a glimpse of the monster. One man, called John Reichart, got more than he bargained for when driving through the nature reserve. The creature leaped on to his car bonnet and the only way John could shake it off was by driving into a tree.

The police investigated and decided it was just teenagers dressing up in gorilla costumes playing pranks, but not everyone was convinced. Could teenagers really kill sheep and hurl heavy car wheels?

## THE BEAST OF GÉVAUDAN

Almost 300 years ago, in the remote mountains of Gévaudan in the south of France, villagers were terrified by a murderous monster that lurked deep in the forest.

VILLAGERS WERE TERRIFIED BY A MURDEROUS MONSTER LURKING IN THE FOREST.

The first victim was a 14-year-old girl, who was attacked while looking after her sheep. Over 100 more deaths followed. Witnesses described a wolf-like animal, with a broad chest, a long thin tail, huge paws and deadly fangs. It could also jump vast distances. Whatever it was, it needed to be stopped.

Hunters took up the challenge and killed hundreds of wolves, but the attacks continued. Finally, a local farmer, Jean Chastel, managed to corner a great beast and shoot it dead. So what was the creature? Frustratingly, the records don't say. Perhaps it was simply a large wolf, but some wildlife experts believe the description sounds like a lion. Lions, unlike wolves, have a thin tail, large paws and can bound great distances. But what was a lion doing in France in the 1700s?

# DEMONS AND DEVILS

With so many sightings of strange creatures around the world, can all of them really be cases of mistaken identity?

## THE JERSEY DEVIL

The Jersey Devil lives deep in the woods of the Pine Barrens in New Jersey, USA. The story goes that 300 years ago, a poor peasant woman discovered she was to have a 13th child. She had no way to feed yet another baby, so she cursed the child.

Months later, the baby was born. For a moment, all seemed well, but within minutes the boy transformed before his mother's eyes. He started to grow at amazing speed, horns burst through his head and his fingers became talon-like claws. Leathery wings sprang from his back and his skin sprouted fur and feathers. His eyes glowed red and sharp fangs glistened in his mouth. The creature attacked his family and ran into the woods, where it's said he still roams to this day . . .

## VEGETABLE MAN

Late one evening in the summer of 1968, Jennings Frederick was out hunting in the countryside of West Virginia, USA, when something very odd appeared before him: a figure with a green stalk-like body and twig-thin arms, and a face with slanted eyes and long green ears.

IT LOOKED JUST LIKE A HUMAN STICK OF CELERY!

Then Jennings noticed this extraordinary creature's hands. Each 'finger' had a strange suction device at the end and, in place of a fingernail, a long sharp needle. Before Jennings could say or do anything, it pushed one of the needles into his hand and began taking his blood! A minute later, the creature's eyes turned from yellow to red and it leaped up a nearby hillside, never to be seen again.

## MOTHMAN

In November 1966 in West Virginia, USA, Roger and Linda Scarberry and Steve and Mary Mallette were driving home from a night out together. Suddenly, a two-metre-high moth-like creature with glowing red eyes began hovering over their car. Terrified, they drove faster and faster but the weird winged being had no problem keeping up.

Eventually, the creature flew away, but the friends reported the incident to police and the story made the newspapers. It became clear the two couples weren't alone. Plenty of people had seen this thing but were too embarrassed to mention it, for fear of being laughed at. Over the next year there were over 100 more sightings.

These continued until a dreadful accident happened in the area. A bridge collapsed, killing 46 people. After this, the creature was never seen again in West Virginia. However, the same mothman was spotted around the world just before other disasters happened – nuclear accidents, outbreaks of disease and even other bridge collapses. It's made people wonder . . . can the mothman predict tragedy? If so, it's even more reason to be worried if you ever spot him.

# PICTURE PERFECT

A picture is worth a thousand words . . . but what if that picture is a fake?

## THE COTTINGLEY FAIRIES

About 100 years ago, in Cottingley in the north of England, two young cousins did something extraordinary. Frances and Elsie managed to take photos of the fairies that played at the bottom of their garden.

When Elsie's mother saw the pictures, she was amazed. The fairies were clearly visible, dancing in front of the girls. She showed the photos to an expert, who was also astonished, and declared the images genuine.

Soon it seemed like the whole country was talking about the fairies. Newspaper articles and books were written about them, and people travelled to Cottingley to hear the cousins' story.

The trouble was, it was all fake.

Some weeks earlier, the girls had told their parents they had found fairies in the garden but were cross when they weren't believed. They set out to prove the grown-ups wrong and placed some fairies they had drawn in the grass and started taking pictures.

However, what began as a prank turned into a very big news story. You can imagine how the girls felt when everyone started to believe them! Very quickly, it became impossible for them to admit what really happened without getting into trouble, so the two cousins played along for years.

After she grew up, Elsie did admit that the photos were a hoax. However, the last time Frances ever spoke about the pictures, just before she died in 1986, she insisted that although they faked most of the pictures, one of them was real . . .

## THE SURGEON'S PHOTOGRAPH

There have been stories of a monster in the deep dark waters of Loch Ness, a great lake in Scotland, for centuries. But in the 1930s, there was a buzz of excitement about a photograph of the Loch Ness monster, which was published in a British newspaper. Today, the image is known as the 'surgeon's photograph'.

The picture was taken in 1934. It's black and white and a little smudged, but you can clearly see the shape of a monster's long neck poking out of the water. Had 'Nessie' been captured on camera? Many people thought so. The photograph was taken by a respectable London surgeon, Robert Kenneth Wilson. No one could imagine he would lie. If the doctor said the photo was real, it was real.

SIXTY YEARS LATER, THE TRUTH WAS REVEALED . . .

The photograph was a hoax planned by famous hunter, Marmaduke Wetherell. In 1933, he had been hired by a newspaper to track the monster down. When he had spotted massive footprints around the lake, he thought he'd found Nessie's trail, but the animal prints had been faked. Someone had used a stuffed elephant's foot to trick him! The newspapers made fun of him so, to get revenge, he organised a fake photo, knowing that the newspapers would publish the story.

Wetherell asked Dr Wilson, who was a friend of a friend, to photograph a toy dinosaur floating in the lake. He knew that no one would question the doctor's honesty. And he was right. For years, nobody did. So the most famous Nessie photo ever is a fake. But it's not the only picture of the monster. Are all the others fakes too?

# ANCIENT TUNNELS

Step into passageways of the past . . . but are they really ancient at all?

## TEMPLAR TUNNELS

In 2017, a network of underground arches, corridors and stairways were uncovered in Shropshire, England. But who carved them into the sandstone and why? The discovery made the news because some people thought the caves had once been used by the Knights Templar.

The Knights Templar were a religious group formed in the 1100s. They were like warrior monks on horseback who protected pilgrims travelling from Europe to the Holy Land. The group broke up in the 1300s, but legend has it they became a top-secret organisation to look after special holy relics. Some people still believe there is a hoard of Templar treasure out there somewhere, just waiting to be discovered . . .

So it's no surprise that these passages caused a stir. But is everything quite as it seems? These tunnels are not the only ones in the area. The Hawkstone Follies are close by and include an even bigger underground grotto. We know they were built in the 1700s as a tourist attraction. So are these caves just another quirky folly?

## MARGATE SHELL GROTTO

In 1835, James Newlove was digging a pond near his home in Margate, England, when he discovered a large underground cavern. To find out more, he tied a rope to his son, Joshua, and lowered him into the hole . . . What was down there?

What Joshua saw amazed him – a great underground grotto spectacularly covered with seashells.

James soon discovered a circular chamber with a domed ceiling and a corridor leading to a smaller room with what looked like a church's altar built into it. Every inch of wall was covered in shells, placed carefully in shapes and patterns – there were owls, crocodiles, turtles, skeletons and more.

HOW DID THEY GET HERE? NO ONE KNOWS.

Researchers later counted over four million shells in the grotto. Some were from the Margate seaside, but some were from as far away as the Caribbean. How had they got here?

To this day, no one knows who created this extraordinary hideaway, and even working out when it was built is difficult. After it was discovered, it became a popular tourist attraction. Gas lamps lit up the passages but covered the shells with soot, making it hard for archaeologists to date them.

So why might it have been built? Some people believe it was for an ancient secret religious group, a hiding place for magicians, or even the Knights Templar once again. Others think it's just a hoax, but so far there are no real answers . . .

# DUPES AND DECEPTIONS

Even when we're told something's a lie, we don't always believe it!

## PILTDOWN MAN

In 1912, amateur archaeologist Charles Dawson made an amazing discovery close to the village of Piltdown in the south of England: an ancient skull, some teeth and a jawbone. He took them to the British Museum to show fossil expert Arthur Woodward.

Arthur was astonished. He believed Charles had uncovered the remains of an early human ancestor, which could be half a million years old. Not only that, the skull was unlike any ever found before. It showed a moment in our evolution when humans developed from apes, the so-called 'missing link'. 'Piltdown man', as it became known, was a massive discovery.

But, in 1949, the skull was examined again with new technology that could date bones more accurately. This revealed the skull wasn't 500,000 years old, but 500. Not only that, the skull and jawbone actually came from different species – human and ape – and the ape teeth had been filed down to make them look more like human teeth. The bones had even been stained to make them appear older.

IT WAS A DARING FRAUD, BUT WHO WAS TO BLAME?

Charles was the chief suspect, but he had long since died. Some years later, an old box was found in the British Museum stores. Inside it were more bones, stained in exactly the same way as the Piltdown skull. Had these bones been a test run? Was someone at the museum the fraudster?

## THE PACIFIC NORTHWEST TREE OCTOPUS

It was 1998 when the world first learned that the Pacific Northwest tree octopus was in danger. A professional-looking website, with links to videos of tree octopuses hatching, explained how the creature, found in Washington State, USA, was now almost extinct.

The website was a hoax, created by a known practical joker Lyle Zapato. However, a later study into what people believe on the internet revealed that almost 90 per cent of 13-year-olds who visited the site believed the octopus was real.

THE TREE OCTOPUS WAS ALMOST EXTINCT.

The website looked convincing and well researched, and that was enough for most teenagers to accept it was a real story. The study highlighted the need to teach people not to assume everything they read online is true.

## THE RAMBLING ROCKS

In October 1867, a newspaper in Nevada, USA, published an article by Dan de Quille, a writer well known for his funny made-up stories. The late 1800s were a time of incredible scientific discoveries and Dan's articles poked fun at the never-ending list of amazing new finds. His latest story told the tale of some extraordinary rocks in the Pahranagat mountains in Nevada. These rocks couldn't stay apart. When placed on a level surface, they always rolled towards each other.

However, the spoof article was reprinted by other newspapers around the world . . . and before long readers were demanding more details. Dan was even offered huge amounts of money to go on tour with his incredible rocks. When he insisted that he had made the whole story up, scientists around the world refused to believe him. They thought he was trying to keep an amazing scientific discovery to himself!

Twelve years after the original article, Dan was still receiving letters about the stones and despite publishing another article confirming the story was a hoax, still not everyone believed him!

# COUNTRIES THAT DON'T EXIST

These places once appeared on maps . . . but where are they really?

## HY-BRASIL

For over 400 years until the 1800s, a tiny island named Hy-Brasil could be found on maps, off the west coast of Ireland. Today, we know no such island exists, but even when it was plotted on sailors' charts, few people ever saw it. That's because Hy-Brasil was said to be completely hidden by mist except for just one day every seven years.

IT WAS SAID TO BE HIDDEN BY MIST EXCEPT FOR ONE DAY EVERY SEVEN YEARS.

However in 1647 a Scottish sea captain called John Nisbet claimed not only to have spotted Hy-Brasil but to have landed on it too. He said the place was overrun with large black rabbits. The sailors were greeted by a magician who lived in a stone castle and a wise old man who gave them gifts of gold and silver.

Some years later, the island had another visitor, T. J. Westropp, an Irish historian. He was so enchanted by the place he returned three times and even took his family on holiday there! Each time the island seemed to appear out of thin air on his arrival and disappear as he left.

Many people have tried to explain how explorers could visit an island that today clearly doesn't exist. In this area, an underwater rock shelf known as Porcupine Bank makes the Atlantic Ocean very shallow. During the last ice age, sea levels fell as water turned to snow and ice. So had Porcupine Bank become the mythical island of Hy-Brasil?

Perhaps . . . except the last ice age ended around 12,000 years ago, way before explorers claimed to have been there.

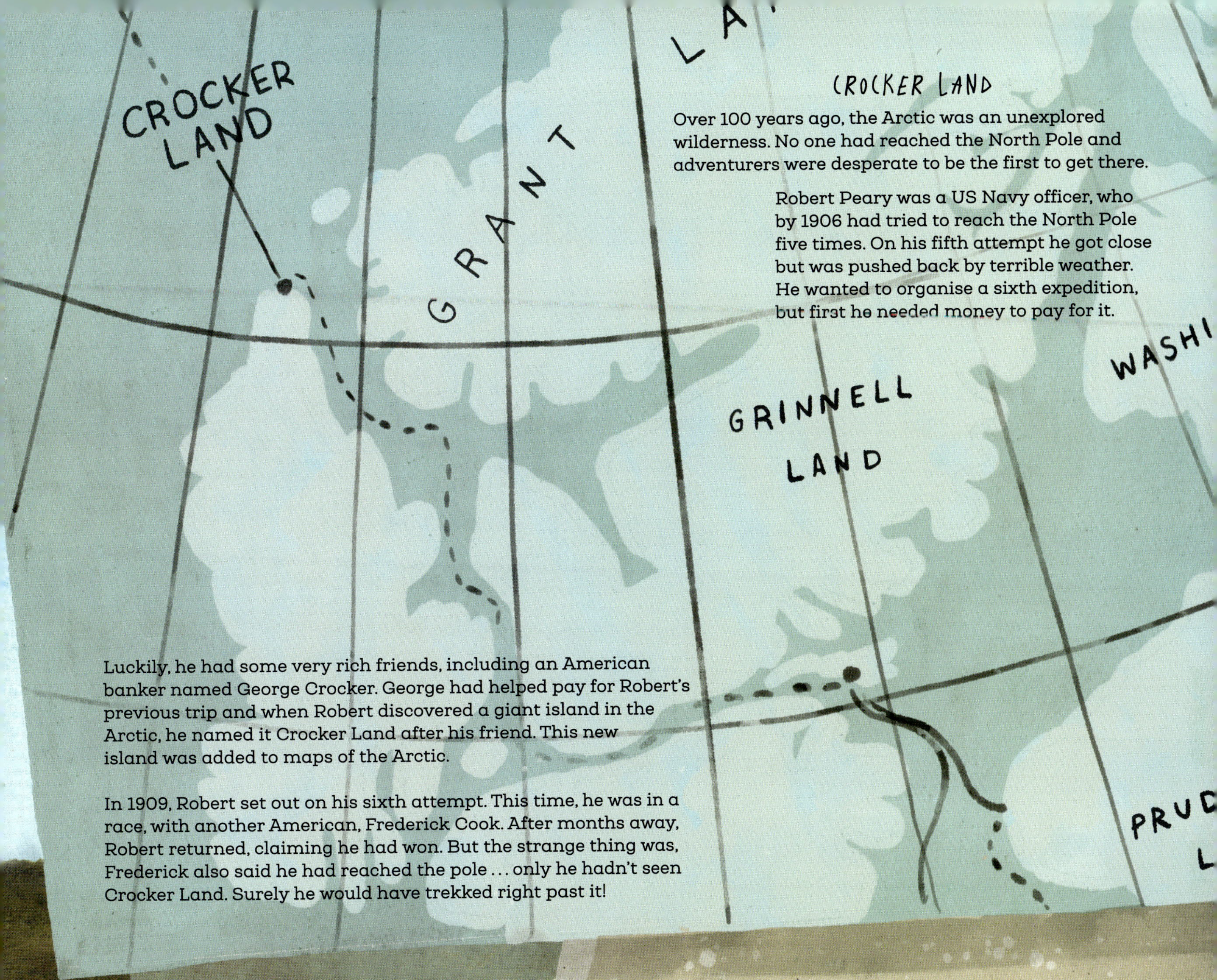


## CROCKER LAND

Over 100 years ago, the Arctic was an unexplored wilderness. No one had reached the North Pole and adventurers were desperate to be the first to get there.

Robert Peary was a US Navy officer, who by 1906 had tried to reach the North Pole five times. On his fifth attempt he got close but was pushed back by terrible weather. He wanted to organise a sixth expedition, but first he needed money to pay for it.

Luckily, he had some very rich friends, including an American banker named George Crocker. George had helped pay for Robert's previous trip and when Robert discovered a giant island in the Arctic, he named it Crocker Land after his friend. This new island was added to maps of the Arctic.

In 1909, Robert set out on his sixth attempt. This time, he was in a race, with another American, Frederick Cook. After months away, Robert returned, claiming he had won. But the strange thing was, Frederick also said he had reached the pole . . . only he hadn't seen Crocker Land. Surely he would have trekked right past it!

To clear up the confusion, a third explorer, Donald MacMillan set off to find the mystery island in 1913. When Donald returned, four years later, he had some surprising news. Crocker Land was nowhere to be found.

So what was going on? Had Robert made up Crocker Land so that other rich people might support his trips to get islands named after them? We can't be sure, but it sounds quite likely.

# CITIES BENEATH THE WAVES

Fantastical stories of extraordinary cities . . . but where are they now?

## ATLANTIS

Over 2,000 years ago, the Greek writer Plato wrote about a great city on an island in the Atlantic. The city, Atlantis, had existed thousands of years earlier. It was home to a group of superhumans, who had built an amazing civilisation on an island rich with wildlife, gems and precious metals. Then, a mysterious disaster hit and the city vanished, never to be seen again.

At first, people thought Plato's story was an allegory – a story with a hidden meaning. They believed Plato made it up to show how pride comes before a fall. The people of Atlantis thought themselves so special that they became smug and the gods taught them a lesson by destroying their city. But hundreds of years later, people began to wonder . . . Had it been a real city after all?

People have searched everywhere for the Atlantis, from the Straits of Gibraltar to the Azores, from the island of Crete to Tenerife. However, we're still no closer to knowing where – if it exists – Atlantis might be.

Occasionally, possible clues are found. Some years ago, off the coast of Bimini, an island in the Bahamas, something that looked like a man-made road was discovered. Huge rectangular blocks of limestone run in a straight line for almost a kilometre, with raised pavements on either side. While geologists believe this is an unusual but natural rock formation, some wonder if this could be the remains of Atlantis.

Although no definite evidence has ever been unearthed, there's a lot under the waves still to discover. Who knows what might be found in the future?

# VINETA

Atlantis isn't the only city lost to the oceans. Somewhere in the dark icy waters of the Baltic Sea is another historical paradise, Vineta. A thousand years ago, Vineta was said to be a fabulously wealthy city on an island. The shops were filled with the finest goods and the people dressed in the most beautiful outfits. Even the children's toys were made of gold and silver! But the people started behaving badly, so the gods took action.

A mermaid was sent to warn the people of their doom, but no one listened. They were too busy enjoying themselves. The wise elders tried to persuade the young people to leave the city, but again, their warnings were ignored. Eventually the gods lost patience with the people and sent a huge storm and the city was swallowed up by the Baltic Sea.

## BUT WHERE IS THE LOST CITY TODAY?

Some people believe that Vineta is near the Polish island of Wolin on the Baltic coast. Here, pillars and what could be the remains of buildings are said to stretch into the sea. Some say that when the waters are calm, occasionally, ghostly figures can be seen walking the flooded streets …

# THE HANGING GARDENS OF BABYLON

It was one of the Seven Wonders of the Ancient World, but where has it gone?

Two thousand years ago, ancient Greek writers listed seven of the most extraordinary structures from the Mediterranean and Middle East. These became known as the Seven Wonders of the World.

In Egypt, there was the Great Pyramid of Giza and the famous lighthouse at Alexandria. At Olympia in Greece there was a giant ivory statue of the god Zeus. In Turkey, there was the magnificent temple for the god Artemis and the huge tomb of King Mausolus, decorated with hundreds of life-sized figures. On Rhodes, there was the Colossus – a massive bronze statue in the harbour. Finally, there were the Hanging Gardens of Babylon, incredible gardens built on raised terraces, that appeared to 'hang' in the air.

The Great Pyramid is still standing today, and evidence has been found for five more of the Wonders, which allow us to pinpoint them exactly. But little is known about the Hanging Gardens.

## DID THEY REALLY EXIST? AND IF SO, WHERE?

The ancient city of Babylon was in modern-day Iraq, and plenty of fabulous remains of the city have been uncovered there. Many believe if they did exist, the Hanging Gardens were built by King Nebuchadnezzar II, over 2,500 years ago. Nebuchadnezzar's wife, Amytis, missed the green hills of her homeland, so perhaps the king built a garden to remind her of home?

Certainly Nebuchadnezzar liked to build. He constructed temples and palaces across Babylon, creating one of the most spectacular cities of the ancient world. But he kept written records that have since been found ... and there's no mention of any gardens. So why does anyone think these gardens were ever real? It's because some classical authors described the Seven Wonders in detail. Six of these structures were actually built, so it seems strange that they would mention a seventh, the gardens, if they didn't exist.

But how was it even possible to grow a garden in the heat of the Babylonian sun, 2,500 years ago? Over the years, archaeologists working on sites in Babylon have found bricks with Nebuchadnezzar's name inscribed on them, covered in bitumen. This is a tar-like waterproof substance that would have stopped water soaking through the brick – perfect for building flower beds or anything else designed to keep water in. A water supply, the River Euphrates, ran close by, and this water could have been raised up to these waterproof terraces with a clever device called an Archimedes screw.

So, it's possible that the Hanging Gardens did once exist, but until more evidence is found ...

IT REMAINS ONE
OF THE GREATEST
MYSTERIES OF
ALL TIME.

# LOST CITIES

Are they lost? Or are they just imaginary?

## EL DORADO

Four hundred years ago, European explorers returned from South America with stories of extraordinary golden cities deep in the rainforests. One explorer, Juan Rodríguez Freyle, wrote about a community who sprinkled their leader in gold dust before he paddled a jewelled raft across a lake and threw golden treasures into the water as offerings to the gods. Freyle called the leader 'the golden one', or el *hombre dorado* and when he told the story back home, it soon grew.

THE MYSTERIOUS CITIES OF GOLD WERE NOWHERE TO BE FOUND.

El Dorado first became the name of a mythical city . . . then a whole kingdom.

Other explorers returned to Europe with their own tales of golden cities. Alongside El Dorado, there was the Lost City of Z, Quivira, La Canela, Paititi and more. Europe was gripped by gold fever and explorers hunted high and low, hoping to make their fortune . . . but the mysterious cities of gold were nowhere to be found.

Today, adventurers still head into the rainforests of the Americas. They're certain there must be cities hidden there and use laser technology to peer beneath the leaves and branches. Perhaps this new approach will one day uncover the truth about El Dorado . . .

## LIBERTATIA

Imagine an island that's home to hundreds of pirates, with swashbuckling swordfights and walking the plank. A terrifying thought? Well, if the stories are true, it turns out Libertatia was actually a rather pleasant place.

According to a book written in 1726, Libertatia, near Madagascar, was where a band of pirates lived in peace and harmony. *A General History of the Pyrates* was written by Captain Charles Johnson and it reveals that the island was set up by Captain James Mission, a French pirate. He wanted to create a place where everyone was free and equal.

### THE PIRATES LIVED TOGETHER IN PEACE AND HARMONY.

James persuaded other pirates to join him. They built a town, grew crops, farmed animals and even set up a fair way of making laws, where every person had a say. For the 1700s, this was a groundbreaking idea.

But did Libertatia ever really exist? The island has never been found and some people believe the author was, in fact, a cover name for another very famous writer, Daniel Defoe. Daniel strongly disagreed with the way England was being ruled at the time, so perhaps he invented the imaginary paradise island as another way to make his voice heard?

Other people disagree. They point out that the book describes many pirates we know really existed, like Blackbeard, Mary Read and Black Bart – and because so much of the book is true, they wonder if the island of Libertatia is real too.

# BURIED TREASURE

Treasure hunters have spent their lives digging for gold . . . hoping to get rich.

## LOST DUTCHMAN'S MINE

Every year, hundreds of hopeful treasure hunters head to the Superstition Mountains in Arizona, USA. For some, the hunt costs them their lives. They are all looking for the Lost Dutchman's Mine, a gold mine rumoured to have been discovered sometime in the 1800s.

One legend tells how a Mexican treasure hunter called Peralta dug huge amounts of gold out of the mine but, while taking it home, he was attacked – and the gold was taken. Some years later, a German prospector named Jacob Waltz, and nicknamed 'the Dutchman', came across a map revealing the location of Peralta's mine.

JACOB KEPT THE WHEREABOUTS OF HIS GOLD MINE A SECRET.

Like Peralta, Jacob became rich but kept the whereabouts of the mine a secret. Then, when he was old and close to death, he described the location to his friend Julia Thomas. Julia spent weeks looking for the mine. She was the first of many treasure hunters who headed into the Superstition Mountains and, while she didn't find gold, at least she lived to tell the tale . . .

Today, prospectors still comb the dangerous mountains looking for the elusive Lost Dutchman's Mine. But is there really treasure and is it worth the risk? No one has made their fortune here yet!

## OAK ISLAND

Off the coast of Nova Scotia, on Canada's Atlantic coast, is Oak Island. It's tiny, covered in forest and looks a lot like the other 300 islands across the bay.

### BUT MANY PEOPLE BELIEVE OAK ISLAND HIDES A SURPRISING SECRET . . .

One night, 200 years ago, a boy named Daniel McGinnis spotted some lights on the island. Investigating the next day, he found a strange ditch with a pulley hanging close by. It looked as if someone had dug a big hole, lowered something heavy into it, then filled it in.

Daniel knew that pirates once hid in these islands. Could it be buried treasure? He and his friends began digging and quickly came across a circular wall that ran deep into the ground – like a well that had been filled with earth. Then, about six metres down, they discovered wooden planks arranged across an underground pit.

But the boys found no treasure, only more earth. They kept going but after days and days of digging, they gave up, exhausted.

However, the story of the Oak Island treasure pit spread fast, and soon others continued the dig. Thirty metres down, a stone tablet was found with unusual symbols carved into it. It convinced the treasure hunters that there was something special to be found. But as they dug even deeper, the pit began to fill with water and even a pump couldn't keep it from flooding.

Today, people are still fascinated by the Oak Island story, and use modern machinery to drill deeper than ever before. And there are hints that something is down there. Traces of parchment, thick wood, cement and even fragments of gold have been discovered, and one expert is said to have translated those strange tablet symbols to read 'Forty feet below, two million pounds are buried', but whether any real treasure lies at the bottom remains to be seen . . .

# THINGS THAT GO BUMP IN THE NIGHT

Do our spirits live on after we die?

### SPEAKING TO THE SPIRITS

Have you ever seen a ghost? Or heard something go bump in the night? Plenty of people have, and many cultures around the world believe our spirits live on after the body dies. But where's the proof?

Humans have been trying to communicate with these spirits for thousands of years. In the 1800s, séances became a popular way of making contact with the dead. A medium – someone who believed they could speak to the spirits – would sit with a group of people in a darkened room. The medium would fall into a trance and connect with the spirits, so people would go to séances to talk to loved ones they had lost.

Many people thought mediums were fakes, but séances did encourage people to investigate the afterlife. Soon, ghost hunting became very popular. Brave adventurers would spend nights in haunted houses, all in the name of science!

THE MEDIUM WOULD FALL INTO A TRANCE AND CONNECT WITH THE SPIRITS.

They'd study inexplicable patches of cold air, strange balls of light, mysterious visions and unearthly noises. From this they made a list of different types of ghost. One of the most common was called a 'crisis apparition'. This was the ghost of a loved one, seen shortly after that person had died. It's as if their spirit came to say goodbye before it moved on to the afterlife.

But the most dramatic ghost they describe had to be the poltergeist. Usually unseen, poltergeists make weird things happen around a house – doors slam, lights switch on and off, plates and bowls fly out of cupboards. One of the most famous ghost hunters of the 1800s, Sir William Barrett, described meeting a poltergeist in a farmhouse in Derrygonnelly, Ireland in 1877 ...

## THE DEMON OF DERRYGONNELLY

A farmer and his five children weren't sleeping well. For nights on end, bangs and scratches were heard throughout the house. They thought it might be rats, but when none were found no one could understand what was going on. Then objects began to move. Candles and boots would be thrown out of windows, without anyone having touched them.

The farmer was told to leave a Bible on the kitchen table overnight, its pages held open with stones. The next morning, the stones were gone and the Bible was ripped to pieces. Now the family were really terrified. They kept candles lit all night, hoping to keep demons away.

BANGS AND SCRATCHES WERE HEARD THROUGHOUT THE HOUSE ... THEN OBJECTS BEGAN TO MOVE.

Sir William Barrett came to investigate. Finding no explanation for the disturbances, he decided it must be a poltergeist. He discovered he could communicate with the spirit by knocking. If he knocked on a wall once, the spirit would knock back. Twice ... two knocks back. If he knocked five times, the ghoul responded with another five.

Barrett discovered he only had to think about knocking, and the poltergeist responded with the same number of knocks. The spirit could read his mind! So Barrett brought a priest to the house to recite the Lord's Prayer. The ghost made a tremendous din, knocking, scraping and scratching. But, as the priest prayed, the poltergeist stopped protesting and the noise died away. Finally, the spirit was gone. The farmer cried with relief and the family could sleep easily again.

# HAUNTED HOUSES

From humble dwellings to grand palaces, nowhere's safe from a haunting.

## MARIE ANTOINETTE'S GHOST

One hot day in August 1901, two women, Charlotte Anne Moberly and Eleanor Jourdain, spent the day looking around the Palace of Versailles in France. The palace had been French king Louis XVI's home. He and his queen, Marie Antoinette, had lived here until the French Revolution in 1789. Both of them were eventually killed by the revolutionaries.

The two women strolled through the gardens on this perfect summer's day, but soon found themselves lost in the huge grounds. When they passed a deserted farmhouse, the sky and trees appeared to lose their sparkle, even on this glorious day. There was something very odd about the gardens here.

BOTH WOMEN FELT A SHIVER DOWN THEIR SPINES.

Even more strangely, the women kept bumping into people wearing old-fashioned clothes. The palace sometimes hired actors to dress up in period outfits, but these actors were very realistic. They met three palace gardeners, all wearing long frock coats and three-cornered hats. Over a bridge, Charlotte saw a woman sitting sketching. She had blonde curls and was dressed in an antique summer frock.

Some days later, Charlotte and Eleanor discovered something that set their hearts racing. The palace had hired no actors on the day of their visit. Even more extraordinarily, examining paintings of the king and his courtiers, they recognised people they had encountered on their walk. And the lady they'd seen sketching? It was none other than Marie Antoinette.

## THE ENFIELD POLTERGEIST

The Enfield poltergeist is the name given to one of the most well-studied and famous hauntings in history. It began on 31 August 1977, in a very ordinary house in Enfield in London, England. That night, when Peggy Hodgson was putting her children to bed, she heard dreadful scraping noises from the bedroom. A chest of drawers was sliding across the floor. In their beds, 11-year-old Janet and her brother Johnny stared at the chest, horrified.

Peggy tried to push the chest of drawers back but couldn't. Someone – or something – was holding it firm. Then the knocking began – bangs on the wall, on the ceiling, under the floor. Terrified, Peggy called the police. The first police officer to arrive didn't take the family's claims seriously until they saw a chair begin to float!

That night was just the beginning. Over the next two years, the ghostly goings-on just wouldn't stop. Flying chairs, toy bricks, marbles . . . Janet even claimed she was thrown around by some unseen force.

COULD A POLTERGEIST REALLY BE CAUSING ALL THE TROUBLE?

Ghost-hunter Maurice Gosse came to investigate and discovered occasionally Janet would talk in a strange low voice. This, he believed, was the spirit making itself heard. Amazingly, Gosse recorded an interview with this spirit and came to the conclusion the ghost must be that of a man called Bill Wilkins, who had died in the house years earlier.

Then in late 1979, everything suddenly stopped. No one knows why or how. Except . . . some experts think the unsettling events weren't caused by a poltergeist at all, but could all be explained by some clever tricks played by someone mischievous.

# WE'RE GOING ON A WITCH HUNT

Do witches only exist in fairy tales?

Around 500 years ago, many people in Europe and America were terrified of 'real-life' witches. People believed they worked with the devil and could cast spells on you or your family. If you were having problems, witchcraft was often the reason. Was your child poorly? Witches were to blame. Cows not producing milk? Witches. Stub your toe? Witches.

Witches were so feared that they were hunted out in towns and villages. They weren't easy to spot, though. They didn't wear capes and pointy hats. A witch could be a man, woman or even a child. Someone accused of being a witch had to take tests to prove their innocence . . . or reveal their guilt.

But, once accused, it was very difficult to prove you were not a witch. There were so many tests, you were bound to fail one. Having moles or birthmarks was enough to show you were plotting with the devil. Being thrown into a lake was common – only witches floated so you needed to make sure you sank. You might also be asked to say the Lord's Prayer without any mistakes. If all else failed, there was always torture – which usually persuaded a 'witch' to confess.

DO WITCHES SINK OR SWIM?

Across Europe and America, thousands of people were suspected of being witches. In 1543, in Denmark, a woman called Gyde Spandemager was accused of casting spells on the Danish Navy's ships, found guilty and burned at the stake.

In England in 1612, 10 men and women were arrested and hanged as witches after a shopkeeper was said to have been cursed by them.

FEAR AND PANIC SPREAD LIKE WILDFIRE.

## THE SALEM WITCH TRIALS

The most famous witch hunts of all are the Salem Witch Trials. In 1692, in Salem in Massachusetts, USA, two girls said they had been bewitched. The daughter and niece of the town priest twitched and itched and wailed and screamed. Clearly, this was the devil's work, but who had cast the spell? Three women were accused. Perhaps hoping to avoid torture, one woman confessed. What's more, she said she knew of other witches.

People were desperate to hunt them down, but they were also scared they might be accused themselves. All sensible laws and rules were forgotten in the rush to convict people. The most ridiculous 'evidence' was used as proof – if someone even dreamed you were a witch it was enough to get you arrested.

Over the next 15 months in Salem, over 200 people were convicted of witchcraft. But over time, the people of Salem began to realise that the witch trials couldn't be trusted and innocent people had died. In May 1693, any remaining accused witches were released from prison.

# MASS HYSTERIA

There are some occasions when you really don't want to be one of the gang!

## DEADLY DANCING

One summer's day in 1518 in Strasbourg, now part of France, a woman called Frau Troffea began to dance in the street. No one quite knew why, but soon a crowd gathered, cheering and clapping as she danced. Frau Troffea kept dancing and stayed on her feet right through the night and into the next morning. In fact, Frau Troffea danced for six whole days.

Strange? Certainly. But things got stranger still when others across the city joined in with the jig. First it was just a handful of people, but after a week, dozens were dancing.

The authorities didn't know what to do. Doctors decided the dancing was due to 'hot blood' and the best way to treat it was to let people dance away the mania. Town halls were opened up to provide a place to party, and musicians were paid to play music for the dancers. However, the plan backfired a little, as over 400 people ended up dancing until they could no longer stand.

## LAUGHTER – THE BEST MEDICINE?

In January 1962 in the African country of Tanganyika, now known as Tanzania, three pupils at a girls' boarding school began to giggle. Once they started, they just couldn't stop. And it was catching. Other girls got the giggles too, and before long over half the school was snorting and sniggering uncontrollably. But the laughter didn't last for a few minutes . . .

## . . . IT LASTED FOR DAYS ON END.

The teachers were helpless, the girls were exhausted and lessons were impossible. Eventually, the school had to close. But even this didn't put an end to the giggling fit. It spread to other schools in the area, and it was only after two years that the laughter finally stopped and life returned to normal. But could anything really be that funny?

## TWITCH AND SHOUT

In 2011 in the town of Le Roy in New York, USA, cheerleader Katie Krautwurst awoke from a nap one afternoon to find that her face was twitching uncontrollably. Muscle spasms soon followed, which made her arms and legs jerk furiously. By that evening she was in hospital, strapped to a bed to control her wriggling limbs. The doctors had no idea what could have caused this.

Some days later, Katie's best friend, Thera Sanchez, caught the twitching bug and began stuttering, jerking her head and flinging her arms. Then even more people were affected. Before long, around 20 pupils from Katie's school had tics and twitches that they just couldn't control.

Parents wondered if a toxic chemical spill nearby was to blame, or if there was something in the water. But with no real evidence, they were left scratching their heads. Then, after months, the twitching began to disappear, just as mysteriously as it had started.

## WHAT'S GOING ON?

Experts believe these are all cases of something called 'mass hysteria'. In the same way a yawn can be 'catching' (try yawning in a busy train carriage), certain actions and behaviours can spread from person to person, almost like a virus. But what would cause someone to start twitching, dancing or laughing in the first place? Doctors believe that when someone is under a lot of stress, that mental anxiety can turn into something physical, like a twitch. They call it 'conversion disorder'. If a whole school, town or community is under stress, mass hysteria events can be the result.

# BRAIN POWER

Super-human? Or super-sneaky?

## JUST A MAGIC TRICK?

Magicians seem to do the most extraordinary things, with nothing but the power of their minds. They can bend keys and cutlery, read people's thoughts and even make objects float in mid-air. But magicians admit these are just tricks. However, some people believe that telekinesis – the ability to make something move using just brain power – and telepathy – the power to read someone's mind – really do exist. And others claim to have these amazing powers, making them superhuman.

In the 1970s, a Russian woman, Ninel Kulagina, shocked investigators by apparently making matchsticks move with the power of her brain. Israeli Uri Geller regularly seems to use his mind to bend metal and fix broken watches.

THEY CAN READ PEOPLE'S THOUGHTS AND EVEN MAKE OBJECTS FLOAT.

These superhumans call themselves psychics. If they do have the powers they say they do, it would change our understanding of the world forever. However, many psychics have been shown to be fakes, fooling people with cunning magic tricks.

So are telepathy and telekinesis real? To find out, governments around the world have spent millions of dollars investigating. Over 40 years ago, the US military set up the Stargate Project to see if psychics could find enemy weapons or discover foreign government secrets by reading minds. But after 20 years of mixed results, the project was stopped.

A magician called James Randi continued the hunt for the truth. He offered a prize of a million dollars to anyone who could prove they were psychic. Because Randi was a magician himself, he was very good at spotting when someone might be using magic tricks. The million-dollar prize was on offer for almost 20 years, but nobody was able to claim it.

So telekinesis and telepathy might exist . . . But we do know that our minds are capable of plenty of other strange things that are still not fully understood, like the placebo effect.

## THE PLACEBO EFFECT

A placebo is a medicine that contains no medicine at all! They're used when new medicines are being tested. Here's how . . . One group of patients is given the new drug that's being tested, and a second group is given a placebo. The placebo looks like a real medicine – a pill, tablet or syrup – but has no real drugs inside it. Neither group knows who gets the real medicine and who gets the placebo. By comparing how each group feels over time, reseachers can see how well the new medicine works. However, strangely, those who take the placebo often see their health improve. The placebo seems to work, even though there's no medicine in it! How can that be?

Scientists have found that if a person expects to feel better, very often they will. And if someone is taking medicine, they will expect the medicine to make them feel better. It just shows the strength of the mind. Placebos can help with headaches and other simple aches and pains, but also with much more serious illnesses too.

And it's not only medicines. Fake surgery, where a doctor has pretended to operate on a patient, has also been shown to improve health. But perhaps the weirdest thing about placebos is that when people know they are taking a placebo – not a real medicine – they still get better! What on earth is going on here? Somehow, our brain power is affecting our physical body. Perhaps, one day, we'll discover that superhuman mind powers are real.

# FIRE STARTERS

Can a person burst into flames without warning?

### DR JOHN IRVING BENTLEY

On 5 December 1966, in the small town of Coudersport, Pennsylvania, USA, Don Gosnell, an engineer, set out to read Dr John Irving Bentley's gas meter. The retired doctor was elderly and moved slowly so Don knew if the doctor didn't answer the door immediately, he was to let himself in. Don rang the bell, waited, then headed inside Dr Bentley's house.

To begin with, everything appeared in order. He went down to the basement to take a meter reading, but noticed a funny smell in the air. Was it smoke? He started to search the house to check that everything was OK . . .

But it wasn't.

In the bathroom, Don discovered the remains of a right leg and a foot, still in its slipper. That, and a small pile of ashes was all that remained of Dr Bentley. The good doctor appeared to have burned to death. But bizarrely, apart from a neat hole burned in the bathroom floor, nothing else was damaged. The rest of the bathroom was fine and even the doctor's walking stick was undamaged. How could a body be reduced to ashes, yet the rest of the house remain untouched? It didn't make sense.

## COUNTESS CORNELIA DE BANDI

In April 1731, 62-year-old Cornelia De Bandi from Bologna, Italy, was feeling unwell. The Italian countess retired to her room, where she chatted with her maid before getting ready for bed. The next morning, when the countess didn't appear for breakfast, her maid went to check on her. What she found was horrifying.

On the carpet, between the bed and the window, was a small pile of ashes, three fingers, and the burnt remains of two stockinged feet. Close by, covered in more ash, was an oil lamp. Dark sticky soot clung to all the surfaces. What on earth had happened?

A local priest, Reverend Giuseppe Bianchini, was called to investigate. He came to one conclusion: spontaneous human combustion.

## SPONTANEOUS HUMAN COMBUSTION

When something catches fire without actually being lit by a flame, it's known as spontaneous combustion, and some people believe that's just what happened to these two unfortunate characters. They were reduced to ashes with hardly a scorch mark on the rest of their surroundings.

But can humans spontaneously combust? Those that think so claim there have been over 200 cases over the last 400 years, some as recently as 2010. But how might it happen?

Alcohol could play a part, because our bodies can turn alcohol into a substance that catches fire very easily. Others think methane, a flammable gas we all make in our intestines, can sometimes build up and explode. There are more suggestions – strange magnetic and electrical forces around the body, lightning strikes, even laser beams ... but most serious scientists would say there is a simpler explanation for these tragic deaths.

They believe Dr Bentley and the countess turned into human candles. Their clothes acted like wicks burning their body fat like candle wax. Because the bodies burned slowly, their rooms remained undamaged. But what lit these human candles? It might have been methane or magnetic fields – however, the countess liked to bathe in camphor, a flammable liquid said to ease muscle aches, and an oil lamp was found close by. The doctor liked to smoke a pipe so would have been regularly lighting matches. Did they both simply set fire to themselves accidently?

We will never know. But if these aren't cases of spontaneous human combustion, that's not to say it doesn't exist ... There are still 200 more cases to study!

# CITY IN THE SKY

Building this today would be a mammoth task. So how did our ancestors manage to do it?

Machu Picchu is a hidden city perched high in the mountains of the Peruvian Andes. It was built around 600 years ago by the Inca people and was unknown to the wider world until an American explorer, Hiram Bingham, was shown the incredible remains by a Peruvian guide in 1911.

It was most likely a royal retreat for Incan emperors, where they could relax and entertain guests. However, research suggests it wasn't only for the royals. Incan citizens might have travelled from afar to visit it too.

Building a city on top of a mountain is a difficult job, but the construction of Machu Picchu was doubly impressive, because the area often experiences earthquakes. In fact, experts believe the site was hit by tremors even as the city was being built.

The Incas used a special building method to keep their structures upright. They didn't use mortar to stick stones together as this could become loose during a quake. Instead, they made sure their stones fitted exactly together by cutting them incredibly accurately. Some joints between stones are so tight, it's impossible to squeeze even a sheet of paper into them.

Machu Picchu reveals that the Incas were amazing engineers, but because they had no written language, we may never know what other secrets their extraordinary civilisation might have held.

# HENGES AND GLYPHS

Amazing ancient structures are all around us.
But what were they for, and how were they created?

## STONEHENGE

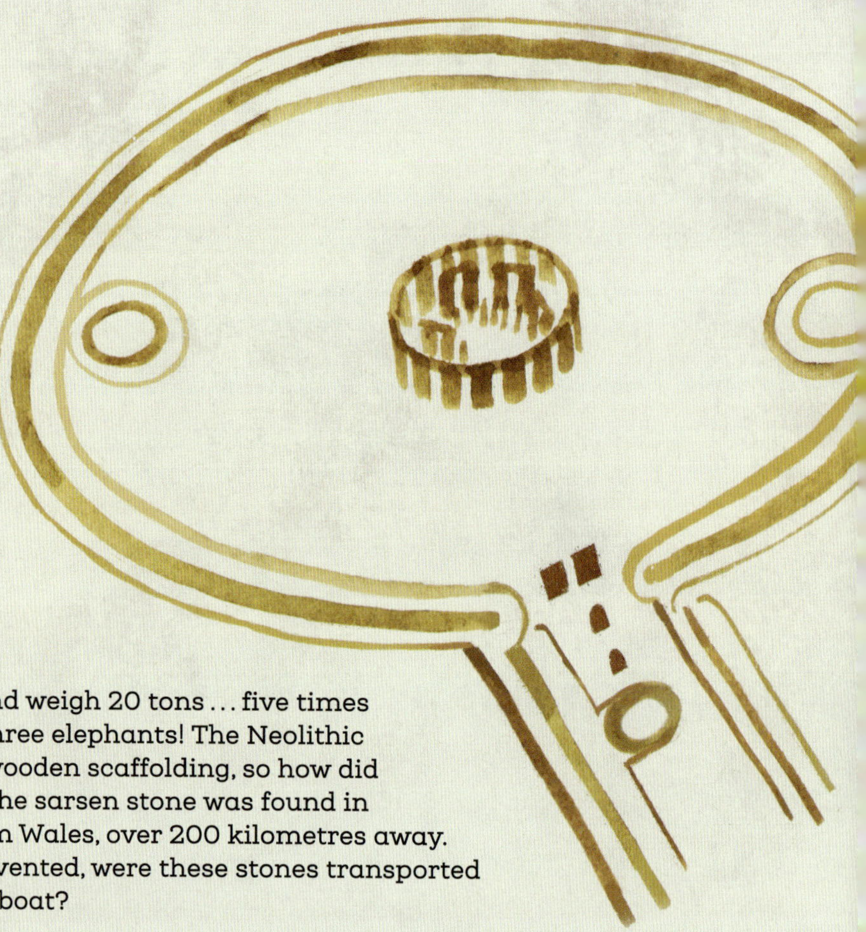

On a flat stretch of Salisbury Plain in southern England sits one of the most extraordinary man-made structures on Earth – Stonehenge. This stone monument is thousands of years old and has baffled archaeologists and engineers for generations. The ancient Neolithic people who built it left no written records, so we still aren't sure how – or why – it was built.

The first structure at Stonehenge is thought to have been a simple stone ring, constructed 5,000 years ago. Over time, more stones were added and the layout was changed. Today, if you visit, you will see the remains of a monument built over 3,500 years ago, when a ring of huge upright stones known as sarsen stones ran around the outside. Inside, there's a ring of smaller stones called bluestones.

The biggest stones are 9 metres high and weigh 20 tons . . . five times taller than an adult and heavier than three elephants! The Neolithic people had only handmade ropes and wooden scaffolding, so how did they lift these giant stones? And while the sarsen stone was found in local quarries, the bluestones came from Wales, over 200 kilometres away. How, when the wheel hadn't yet been invented, were these stones transported here? Were they dragged or brought by boat?

If we knew why Stonehenge was built, it might help us find the answers. Human bones have been discovered here too, so perhaps it was a burial site. More clues come from the stones themselves. At certain times of the year, they come into line with the position of the sun and moon in the sky. Does this mean it was a giant calendar used to signal the changing seasons? Some researchers suggest the bluestones had special healing powers and people might have travelled thousands of kilometres just to touch them.

We may never know how or why this amazing stone circle was built, but the fact it was built at all is incredible!

## THE NAZCA LINES

On the other side of the world lies the remains of another remarkable feat of human engineering. Built 1,500 years after Stonehenge, the Nazca Lines are just as mysterious.

Over an area of 500 square kilometres in the desert plains of southern Peru, almost 400 huge drawings are etched into the ground. These designs in the earth are called geoglyphs. There are pictures of birds, spiders, monkeys and plants, as well as triangles and spirals. Some are as big as the Empire State Building and so large that it's impossible to tell what they are from the ground. It wasn't until archaeologists were able to fly over the area that people realised just how complicated these drawings were.

Creating lines in the dark red earth of the Peruvian desert is simple enough – scraping rocks and stones from the surface reveals the lighter sand underneath. However, drawing something so big – and getting all the proportions, curves and straight lines right – is incredible.

## HOW DID OUR ANCESTORS DO IT?

And what were the Nazca Lines for? All kinds of explanations have been suggested. Perhaps they were another type of ancient calendar, a reflection of the shapes our ancestors saw in the stars, a prayer to the gods to send rain to the scorched desert plains, or even an airstrip for passing spaceships! Until definite proof is found, we can only guess …

# TOMBS AND TUNNELS

These underground structures reveal how our ancestors burrowed and built.

## THE MANDRAKE CAVES OF BAVARIA

One afternoon, young Beate Greithanner was tending her cows in the Bavarian Alps in Germany, when suddenly one of the animals vanished. A hole had opened up beneath the unfortunate creature and swallowed her. What Beate had discovered was an erdstall, a hidden labyrinth of underground tunnels.

Around 700 erdstall have been found beneath Bavaria, and there are more in neighbouring Austria. They're known as 'goblin holes' or 'mandrake caves', named after the mandrake plant, which is thought to have magical powers. The tunnels lie around 10 metres below ground and are up to 50 metres in length, with passages, loops and even chambers big enough to stand upright in.

Researchers say the tunnels are over 1,000 years old but aren't really sure why they were built. They may have simply been places to hide from invaders or a way to communicate with spirits in the underworld. But these theories have yet to be proved, so the erdstall are still mysteriously unexplained.

## THE PLAIN OF JARS

Across hundreds of kilometres of grassland in the Southeast Asian country of Laos lie thousands of ancient stone jars. They're huge – big enough to climb into – weigh as much as 14 tons and are over 1,500 years old.

Legend has it that the stone jars were created by Khun Cheung, the king of a race of giants who once lived here. He used them for brewing drinks to celebrate a victory against a bitter enemy. But what were they really for?

The answer is, no one really knows. Some researchers wonder if the plains are an ancient graveyard, and the jars were used to store the ashes of leaders of the local tribes. Others believe the location of the jars is a clue. They appear to run in a line, like a path through the countryside, so they might be an unusual form of signpost, marking out important routes across the land. Perhaps they even collected rainfall to provide tired travellers with fresh water on their journey.

Until more research is done, the mystery of the jars remains . . .

# LOST BURIAL GROUNDS

They were the biggest names of their age . . .
And yet today they are nowhere to be found.

## QUEEN NEFERTITI

Queen Nefertiti was one of ancient Egypt's most powerful women. She was married to the pharaoh Akhenaten and helped rule the country until her death almost 3,500 years ago. We know she was important because writings by the ancient Egyptians mention her again and again. We even know what she looked like, thanks to a sculpture of her found by archaeologists.

BUT WHERE IS SHE NOW?

Such an important monarch would be expected to have an impressive tomb in Egypt's Valley of the Queens where many other female rulers were buried, but nothing has ever been found. She wasn't buried with Akhenaten either. Some believe she might be buried in a secret chamber in another pharaoh's tomb – Tutankhamun's. But despite years of searching, that chamber – if it exists – remains hidden.

There's a chance that her body has already been found in yet another pharaoh's tomb. An ancient preserved body, known as a mummy, was discovered in Amenhotep II's tomb that had unusual ear piercings. Images of Nefertiti show that she had similar ear piercings. However, not everyone is convinced. This mummy might not even be female, which means Nefertiti's final resting place remains a mystery . . . for now.

## ALEXANDER THE GREAT

Alexander was king of Macedonia almost 2,500 years ago. He travelled across the known world with his army, conquering enemies and building a great empire that stretched from Greece to modern-day Pakistan. At the age of 20, he was respected by his fierce army thanks to his courage and character.

Alexander died aged 32, but today, no one knows where he is buried. When he died, his close friends fought over who should bury his body and it finally ended up in Alexandria, Egypt. We know many famous people – Julius Caesar, Cleopatra, Caligula and Hadrian – visited Alexandria to see his tomb, but we've found nothing that pinpoints where his body lay.

Over the years, it's also got more complicated because Alexandria has been hit by floods and earthquakes. The ground has sunk about three and a half metres since Alexander's time and the ancient city has been rebuilt again and again. There have been over 140 archaeological digs to search for the tomb but, so far, Alexander remains lost.

## GENGHIS KHAN

One of the cruellest leaders in history, Genghis Khan was the warrior king of the huge Mongol Empire, which at one time stretched from eastern Europe to the Sea of Japan. Khan lived around 900 years ago and he and his Mongol armies are famous for terrorising their enemies.

Before he died, Khan demanded his tomb remain hidden and today its location is still unknown. The reason for his secrecy? It's said that he was buried with great treasures, plundered from his bloodthirsty attacks. But how does a leader keep his burial place a secret when he's dead?

Khan's loyal soldiers carried his body to his final resting place, and it's said that they killed anyone they met so nobody could report what they had seen. Once the body was buried, 1,000 horses galloped over the ground to hide any clues. While archaeologists from around the world hunt for the tomb, many Mongolians don't want it to be found, preferring to respect the warrior king's wishes.

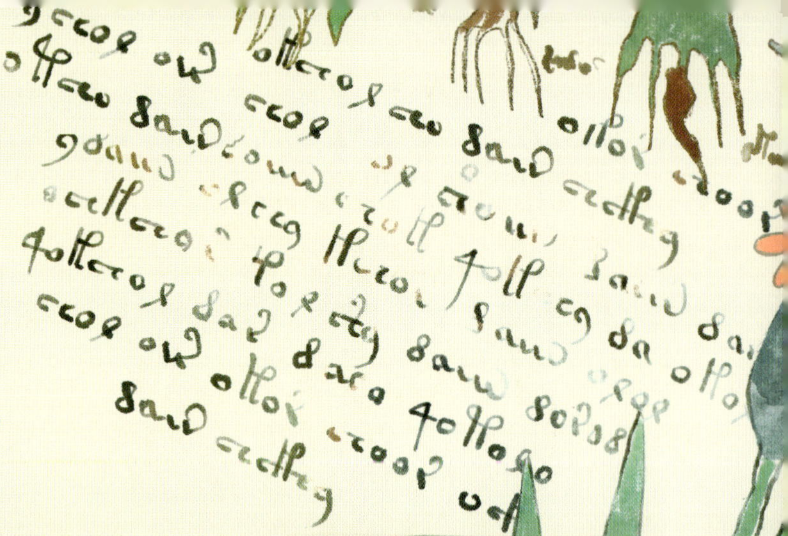

# UNDERSTANDING THE ANCIENT WORLD

## These secret languages are telling us something . . . but what?

As long as we've been able to write things down, we've wanted to keep secrets – from battle plans to love letters – and codes help us do just that. But what if the key to the code goes missing? Here are some ancient puzzles we've not yet been able to crack.

### THE VOYNICH MANUSCRIPT

The Voynich manuscript was discovered when Wilfrid Voynich, a Polish book dealer, bought some books from an Italian priest in 1912. Hidden among the collection was a handwritten document made from animal skins (vellum). It dates from the early 1400s and was most likely written in Italy, but nobody knows who the author is.

IT'S GOT NO TITLE AND WE DON'T UNDERSTAND A SINGLE WORD OF IT.

Beautifully ornate handwriting covers its 240 pages. But not only do we not know what language it is, we don't even recognise any of the letters. Experts don't know if it's a long-forgotten ancient script, a made-up code or just one big hoax.

Alongside the writing are doodles and sketches. There are bizarre plants, people washing and bathing, the night sky and signs of the zodiac. They give a hint as to what the book might be about – medicine, astrology, even recipes – but after more than 100 years of study, no one has yet been able to explain its secrets.

## THE PHAISTOS DISC

In 1908, the Italian archaeologist Luigi Pernier was exploring Bronze Age remains on the Greek island of Crete when he came across a strange disc the size of a side plate. The 3,500-year-old clay disc, later named after the Minoan Palace of Phaistos where it was found, is stamped on both sides with around 240 symbols in a spiral pattern.

There's a head, a glove, a cat, a bird, a tree and many other recognisable objects. The symbols are grouped into around 30 'words', which makes archaeologists think it might be a message. But what does it say?

Some theories suggest it might be a prayer to an earth goddess, a greeting or even musical notes, but most researchers believe we'll only ever be able to translate it if we find something else with the same symbols on. Without the clues to crack the code, the Phaistos Disc remains a lost language from ancient times . . .

## THE SHUGBOROUGH INSCRIPTION

In Staffordshire in the heart of England lies Shugborough Hall, a stunning Georgian mansion built almost 300 years ago by George Anson. It's home to a grand statue that has had historians baffled for many years. The Shepherd's Monument includes an ornate carving of a woman and three shepherds. Below them are eight apparently random letters etched into the stone . . . O, U, O, S, V, A, V and V.

MANY PEOPLE BELIEVE IT'S A RIDDLE, BUT DOES ANYBODY KNOW WHAT IT MEANS?

Some experts think the picture of the shepherds has something to do with the legend of the Knights Templar and that the letters point the way to the Holy Grail. Others wonder if it's a coded love poem to George's wife. It's a puzzle the best codebreakers in the country have attempted to break . . . but so far, the riddle is still unsolved.

# CRYPTIC CIPHERS

Mysterious messages from the past, but do they mean anything today?

## HIDDEN GOLD

In January 1820, Thomas J. Beale checked in to a hotel in Lynchburg, Virginia, USA. When he left, he handed a locked metal box to Robert Morriss, the hotel owner, promising he would soon return to collect it. Robert waited 23 years before deciding Thomas must have died and he opened the box. Inside were three pages of numbers and a note explaining that they revealed the location of buried treasure.

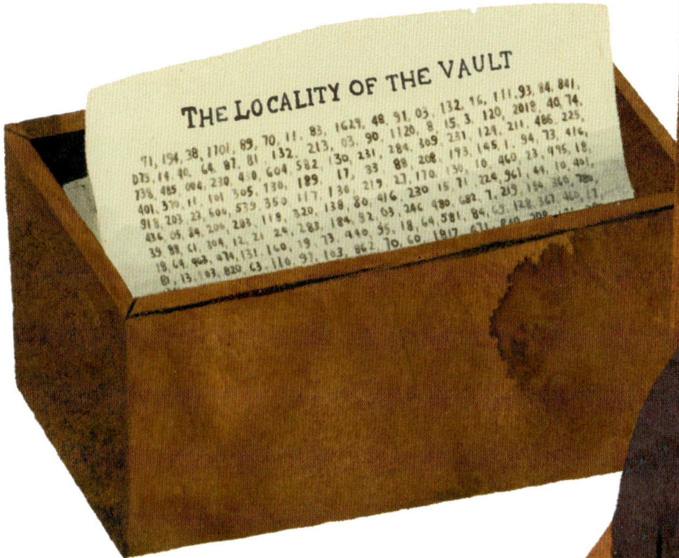

It was a code! Using a secret key or codebook, each number could be swapped for a letter to produce a message in English. But each page used a different code and there was no sign of the codebook.

Miraculously, in the late 1800s, somebody solved one of the pages. The code revealed Thomas had hidden treasure worth 60 million dollars somewhere in the county of Bedford, USA. The exact location is probably hidden within the other two pages . . . but so far no one has managed to crack the two remaining codes!

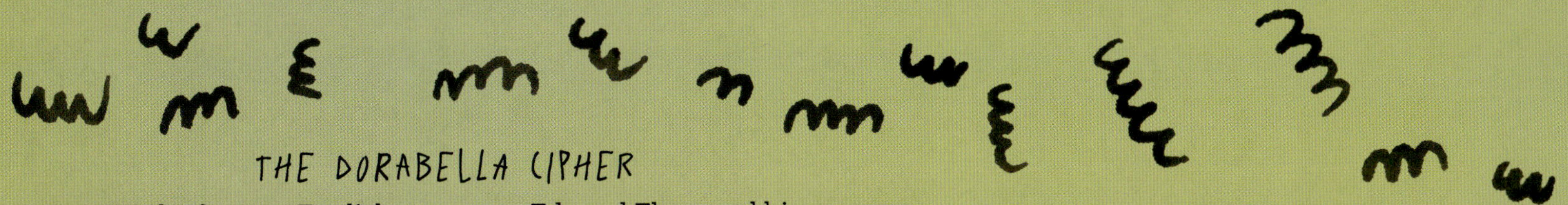

## THE DORABELLA CIPHER

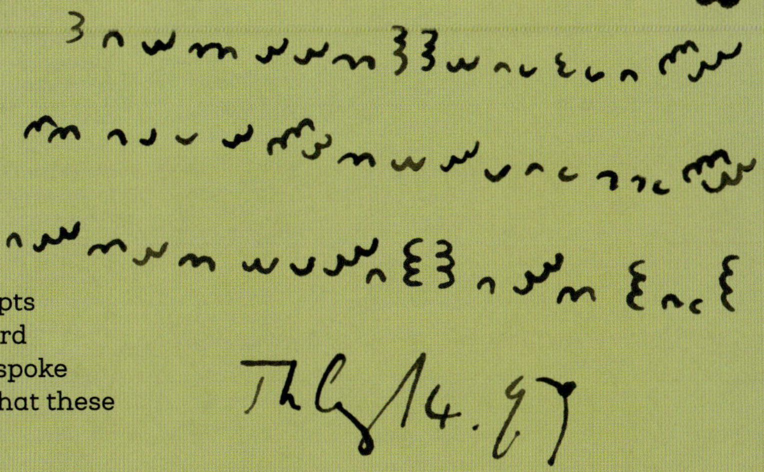

In 1897, the famous English composer Edward Elgar and his wife Caroline stayed with their friends the Penny family for a few days. Afterwards, Caroline sent a thank-you card and included a special note that Edward had written for Dora Penny. But, over 120 years later, the meaning of his message remains a mystery ...

The Dorabella Cipher, as it's known, is 87 characters long. But each character is just a squiggle. What on earth do they mean? The truth is, after all these years and numerous attempts at solving the riddle, nobody knows. But when Dora and Edward were together they often played clever word games and even spoke in their own made-up language, so many people still believe that these squiggly secret symbols are a code worth cracking ...

## THE LOST HOMING PIGEON

In 1982, David Martin was repairing the chimney in his house in Surrey, England, when he came across the delicate skeleton of a bird. The poor animal must have died while trapped in the chimney.

David thought little of it until he noticed a tiny container with the words 'Pigeon Service' strapped to one of its legs. He had discovered the bones of a carrier pigeon. During the Second World War, over 250,000 carrier pigeons were used to send messages hundreds of kilometres, between the battlegrounds and home.

David carefully unscrewed the container's lid. Inside was a handwritten message. It was a collection of 27 five-letter 'words', made of random letters like RQXSR, JRZCQ, CMPNW.

## WHAT DID IT MEAN?

Even GCHQ – the British government's top-secret codebreaking department – was stumped. Perhaps a clue to the message is where the pigeon was found ... halfway between Bletchley Park, where British codebreakers were based during the Second World War, and Normandy, where many Allied troops fought. Was this pigeon taking a vital message to soldiers on the front line?

# CURSE OR COINCIDENCE?

Would you risk your life to wear one of these jewels?

## THE HOPE DIAMOND

The Hope Diamond is a brilliant blue gemstone about the size of a walnut. It weighs over 45 carats, is worth over a quarter of a billion dollars and is named after Thomas Hope, an English author who bought the diamond in 1830. Today, it is on display in Washington DC, USA, but the gemstone has a mysterious past. Some people believe it's cursed and has brought nothing but bad luck to many of its owners . . .

It's said that the diamond once formed the sparkling eye in the head of a statue in an Indian temple, but it was stolen by a thieving priest. It found its way into the hands of a French merchant called Jean-Baptiste Tavernier who sold it to Louis XIV of France in 1668, but was attacked by a pack of dogs soon after! And many others who later owned the stone, including a Russian prince, a Turkish sultan and a Greek princess, also came to a grisly end.

## THE BLACK PRINCE'S RUBY

The Black Prince's Ruby certainly has a very bloody history. In the 1300s, the ruby was owned by the sultan of Granada in Spain, until his arch-enemy, Pedro the Cruel, king of Castile, double-crossed him. The two men met to discuss a peace deal, but making peace was the last thing on Pedro's mind. He killed the sultan and stole the jewel!

Some years later, an English prince known as the Black Prince, son of Edward III, king of England, helped Pedro fight another enemy. Perhaps Pedro had heard rumours of the curse because he handed the ruby to the Black Prince as a gift. But it did neither of them any good! Pedro was killed in battle not long after and the Black Prince went on to suffer a long and lingering death. The prince's son, Richard, inherited the stone and was crowned king of England, but he was soon killed by his successor, Henry IV.

WAS THE STONE BRINGING A TERRIBLE CURSE TO WHOEVER OWNED IT?

## THE KOH-I-NOOR DIAMOND

In 1849, Duleep Singh, the child ruler of the Punjab area of India gave the Koh-i-Noor Diamond to Queen Victoria of Great Britain. Koh-i-Noor means 'Mountain of Light', and it's a stunning stone, but along with the jewel came a 750-year-old curse. It's said that only God and women can wear the diamond without being in grave danger.

Centuries before it came to Britain, the diamond passed from ruler to ruler as wars swept through Asia, and one after another they all came to sticky ends. Even as the gemstone was brought to Britain, it appeared to reveal its mysterious power as disease wiped out many of the ship's crew on the journey over.

Today, the British royal family still own the diamond. It sits in the Queen Mother's Crown, a crown only ever worn by women. Does this mean they believe in the curse?

EACH STONE LEAVES A BLOOD-SOAKED TRAIL THROUGH HISTORY.

### ARE THESE STONES REALLY CURSED?

Can a curious curse actually be blamed for all the death and misfortune in these stories? Cruel leaders have always fought for power, whether precious stones are involved or not, but the mystery remains as to why each of these jewels appears to leave a blood-soaked trail through the history books …

# SNEAKY SKULLDUGGERY

Three different skulls and three very different mysteries.

## MONKEY BUSINESS

Just outside the town of Armagh, in Northern Ireland, are a strange collection of lumps and bumps in the landscape. There's an outer, perfectly circular mound, surrounding two more circular mounds inside it. Circles are rare in nature, so whatever this is, it must be man-made.

In fact, archaeologists have discovered it's the remains of an Iron Age fort built almost 2,500 years ago. We don't know very much about the community who lived here, but when the Romans conquered England they wrote about ferocious people living in the north of Ireland that practised human sacrifice.

BUT IT'S NOT HUMAN BONES FOUND IN THE FORT THAT HAVE PUZZLED ARCHAEOLOGISTS – IT'S AN APE!

The single skull of a Barbary ape was discovered here in 1971. Barbary apes are found in north Africa or Gibraltar – 3,000 kilometres south. There's evidence that these animals were sometimes kept as pets. However, experts also believe that once dead, ape skulls were highly prized and would have been bought and sold across Europe. So was an ape living in wet and windy Northern Ireland over 2,000 years ago, or was this skull simply a valuable trinket?

## ALL CLEAR?

In 1924, explorer Frederick Mitchell-Hedges was in the jungles of Belize in Central America. He was excavating a collapsed Mayan temple thought to be 1,000 years old. Some years later, his daughter Anna revealed to the world an extraordinary object she claimed they had found on that expedition – an exquisite crystal skull carved out of a single piece of clear quartz.

While beautiful, it's said to carry a deadly curse. Anna even called it the 'skull of doom'. Similar skulls have been found across Central America, and some people believe they were made by ancient civilisations thousands of years ago. One prophecy even claims that whoever brings together 13 of these crystal skulls will receive secret knowledge essential for humanity's survival.

COULD THESE SKULLS HAVE UNEXPLAINED SUPERPOWERS?

Not everyone thinks so. Close examination of the crystal suggests these ancient Mayan skulls were, in fact, created with more modern machinery. It appears the history of the 'skull of doom' is anything but crystal clear.

## STICKS AND STONES

Archaeologists have uncovered 400-year-old graves in Drawsko, Poland, and Venice, Italy, with hundreds of dead in them. Some of the skeletons have been found with large stones forced into their mouths. Not only that, their necks are pinned to the ground with sickles – large curved blades used for cutting grasses and grains. What on earth is going on?

These are known as 'vampire burials'. Rocks were sometimes placed in the mouths of the dead to stop them feeding on the living and the blade would cut off their heads as they rose from the grave. Terrifying stuff!

At the time of the burials, large parts of Europe were suffering. Thousands of people were being killed by diseases like the plague. Today, we know the plague was spread by fleas on rats, but in earlier times people did not understand how so many could die. They wondered if vampires were to blame and felt safer if they did everything they could to stop corpses coming back to life …

# AMAZING ANCESTORS

Predicting the future, pots of power and jet planes.
How much did our ancestors know?

## A 2,000-YEAR-OLD COMPUTER

In 1901, a team of divers discovered a 2,000-year-old shipwreck, packed with ancient treasures, off the Greek island of Antikythera. Alongside statues and coins was a lump of metal and wood the size of a shoebox that hid an extraordinary secret. It was a strange clock-like machine, with over 30 bronze interlocking cogs that moved hands and dials on the front and back of the box.

HOW DID OUR ANCESTORS KNOW HOW TO BUILD IT?

It is the most complicated piece of machinery ever found from the ancient world. But what did it do? Experts worked long and hard at trying to understand the machine. Finally, they discovered it was an ancient programmable computer that could predict the position of the sun, moon and planets in the sky, the phases of the moon and dates of solar and lunar eclipses for hundreds of years to come. It could have been used to set dates for religious festivals, crop planting or even when to go to war.

But there is still a mystery that remains unsolved. Nothing this complicated was built for another 1,500 years, when the first clocks were invented, so how did our ancestors know how to build it?

## AN ANCIENT POWER PACK?

Did ancient civilisations have electricity? Some people certainly think they did. An archaeologist, Wilhelm Koenig, made a strange discovery 80 years ago, near Baghdad in modern-day Iraq. He uncovered some terracotta pots, almost 2,000 years old, that each contained a rolled-up copper sheet and an iron rod.

Wilhelm knew that thanks to some clever chemistry, if one of these terracotta pots was filled with an acid, like vinegar, the mixture of metals and acid would generate electricity. When the pots were examined ... traces of vinegar were found! Had Wilhelm discovered the world's oldest electric battery?

If these pots are, in fact, ancient batteries, it would rewrite history because the first battery we know of for sure was created in 1800 by Alessandro Volta in Italy. But what might these ancient power packs be used for? Where did our ancestors get the technology? And why hasn't any other evidence of batteries and electricity ever been found since? And if they're not batteries, what are they?

## TAUGHT TO FLY BY ALIENS?

In the early 1900s, dozens of ancient gold trinkets were found in Colombia, South America. Made by the Quimbaya people, they are known as the Quimbaya artefacts and are around 1,000 years old. Each ornament is just a few centimetres long and intricately crafted, and strangely some look remarkably like tiny little aeroplanes! But how would our ancestors know anything about flying machines? They hadn't been invented then!

And there is something even more remarkable about the aeroplanes. In 1994, three German researchers created large-scale models with engines, and when they tested them, the planes actually flew!

HOW COULD THEY KNOW ANYTHING ABOUT FLYING MACHINES?

So did our ancestors really know how to fly? If so, did they work it out themselves or did a visitor teach them? Some people are convinced that these tiny gold planes are evidence of aliens visiting Earth and showing us how to fly.

It would be incredible if creatures from space had stopped by on Earth, but sadly, archaeologists think it's very unlikely. If aliens did visit, would the Quimbaya have made just a few aeroplane models to remember them by, or would there be temples and statues built in their honour?

And if the models aren't aeroplanes, what are they? Archaeologists think other gold trinkets found with the planes look like insects, frogs and other animals. Surely it's more likely that the planes are, in fact, odd-looking birds or fish?

# GLOSSARY

**ABDUCT**
To take somebody against their will, or kidnap.

**ANCESTOR**
A person you are descended from, who lived many years ago.

**ARCHAEOLOGIST**
A person who studies the past by examining things people made and left behind.

**ARCHIMEDES SCREW**
A simple pump that scoops up water and raises it with the turn of a handle.

**ASTROLOGY**
The study of the movement of the stars in the belief that it affects things that happen to us on Earth.

**ASTRONAUT**
A person who travels into space.

**ASTRONOMER**
A person who studies space, galaxies and the stars.

**ATMOSPHERE**
The air surrounding our Earth or another planet.

**BIOLOGY**
The study of living things.

**CARAT**
A measure of weight for precious stones.

**CHEMISTRY**
The study of how substances interact and combine with each other.

**CHIVALROUS**
To be courteous and charming, usually towards women.

**CIVILISATION**
The culture and way of life of a particular group of people.

**COMPLEX**
A collection of buildings or rooms used for a similar purpose.

**CONSCIOUSNESS**
The awareness you have of yourself and your surroundings.

**DECEPTION**
Making someone believe a lie is a truth.

**DIABASE**
A very hard type of rock, also known as dolerite, that is formed under extreme heat.

**ENGINEER**
A person who designs, builds or maintains engines, machines or structures.

**ENTHUSIAST**
A person who is very interested in a particular subject or hobby.

**EVIDENCE**
Information or facts that help you decide whether something is true.

**EVOLUTION**
The way in which living things have developed from earlier kinds of life on Earth.

**EXTINCT**
When a species dies out.

**FOLKLORE**
Traditional customs and stories belonging to a culture or community.

**FOLLY**
An extravagant building created for show.

**GENUINE**
Something that is truly what it is said to be.

**GEOLOGIST**
A person who studies rocks and earth.

**GLACIER**
A slow-moving river of ice.

**HOAX**
Something designed to trick or fool someone.

**HYPNOTISE**
Putting someone into a trance-like state, where they are not fully awake, yet not asleep.

**INVESTIGATION**
Examining something or someone in an organised way to find something out.

**LABYRINTH**
A complicated network of interconnecting tunnels and passages.

**LEGEND**
A historical story that many people believe is true but which there is no evidence for.

**LOGIC**
A way of thinking that breaks a complicated idea down into a series of simpler ideas.

**LORD'S PRAYER**
A prayer, according to the Christian Bible, that Jesus taught his disciples.

**MEDIEVAL**
A time in European history known as the Middle Ages, from around 500 to 1500.

**METEORITE**
A piece of rock that has fallen to Earth from space.

**MICROBE**
A tiny living creature, often only one cell big.

**MILITARY**
A country's armed forces, including the army, navy and air force.

**MINERAL**
Naturally occurring solids made of either a single element, like copper, or a combination, like quartz, that make up rocks and soils.

**MIRACLE**
An event that cannot be explained by the laws of nature as we understand them today, so thought to have a supernatural cause.

**MOLECULE**
Two or more atoms joined together.

**MONUMENT**
A statue or structure built to mark an event or place.

**MYTH**
A traditional story passed down through the ages that uses the supernatural to explain an event or phenomenon.

**NEOLITHIC**
A prehistoric period of the late Stone Age.

**ORGANISM**
Any living thing, but often relating to minute plants and animals.

**PARTICLE**
A tiny piece of matter.

**PHENOMENON**
An unusual event or something that you can see exists but are unable to explain why.

**PHYSICS**
The study of matter and energy.

**PRANKSTER**
A person who plays tricks on others.

**PROOF**
A list of evidence used to show that something is true.

**PROPHECY**
A prediction about something happening in the future.

**PSYCHIC**
A person with powers that can't be explained by science, like being able to read minds.

**PUBLICITY STUNT**
An event that captures the public's attention in order to advertise something.

**RADIATION**
A way in which energy is moved from one place to another, such as heat and light.

**RELIC**
A precious object from an earlier time.

**SETTLEMENT**
Somewhere a group of people create a place to live

**SONAR**
A way of searching underwater using sound waves.

**SPRITE**
An elf or fairy.

**SUPERNATURAL**
Something that can't be explained by the laws of nature, such as ghosts.

**SUPERSTITION**
A belief that has no logical explanation in science but depends on magic or luck.

**TECHNOLOGY**
Using scientific knowledge to solve problems.

**THEORY**
A way of explaining how something happens.

**TOURIST**
A person visiting a place for fun.

**ZODIAC**
A diagram used by astrologers to represent the strip of space in which the sun appears to circle the Earth, which includes positions of the planets and the stars. It is divided into 12 sections, each with its own name and symbol, such as Aries the Ram.

# INDEX